For my beloved Unity
of Gainesville, where so much
of my spiritual life
was fertilized & fed

Love,
Sallee

I

"I know the plans I have for your life, declares the Lord-- plans for welfare and not for calamity, to give you a future and a hope."

God
(Jeremiah 29:11)

The Twelve Disciples

of

A Wild Woman

A Journal Adventure

Sallee Wade

Copyright © 2010 by Sallee Wade

All Rights Reserved. No part of this book may be reproduced in any manner whatsoever without written permission, except in the case of brief quotations. For information contact salleewade@gmail.com.

Cover designed by Chuck Boydstun.
Photo of my Georgia woodstove by Richard Harrison

ISBN: 1456371258

Primary Category – Body, Mind & Spirit/Spirituality/General

EAN – 13   9781456371258
Title ID – 3477121

Printed in the United States of America

The Twelve Disciples
Of
A Wild Woman

A Journal Adventure
Sallee Wade

This book is lovingly and gratefully dedicated
to:
The Unity Church
of
Gainesville, GA.

You gave wings to the roots
Of my relationship with God,
With my Self,
My work in the world,
and
With those I love

Acknowledgements

It takes a 'family of grace' to birth a book. This family is comprised of those who have believed in me, and helped in ways I now see as raw evidence of God's love and grace.

I am deeply indebted to Sarah Quigley, author of *Facing Fear and Finding Courage,* and its second edition, *The Little Book of Courage.* While living in Georgia Sarah (and her husband, Jack), came to my yoga classes. Sarah asked to see what I was writing. After combing through a huge stack of my unwieldy early work, she sent me a lovely greeting card. Fearing rejection, I was afraid to open it. When finally I did, it was full of praise. I still have it framed. Sarah has diligently encouraged my writing, been friend to my soul, and generously supervised the final edit of this manuscript.

I'm equally indebted to Chuck Boydstun, the tool man, computer geek and playmate in my life. His design of the book cover, his unstinting preparation and formatting of this manuscript, his help in proof reading, his being ever at the other end of his cell phone when I'm stuck in a computer glitch - has been a humbling blessing. Throughout this process, he's remained steady during my bouts of cranky frustration and several major meltdowns. (He's also an amazing plumber, does basic wiring, can hang a door and regularly takes me to the symphony).

I'm deeply grateful to Cynthia Brown, the horseback riding pal of my youth and soul sister in our later years. Along with soulful conversations over tea, her eagle eyes as a tireless proof reader and quiet, steady support of my writing have kept me going.

I'm grateful beyond measure to the Unity Church of Gainesville, Georgia, where I first learned about Unity beliefs, and for all the Unity Churches in and around Atlanta, in Chattanooga, Peoria and Quincy Illinois, who have welcomed me as seminar leader and/or Sunday speaker. I'm deeply grateful for Silent Unity's 24 hour prayer line, which I use often, and for the *Daily Word,* my constant devotional companion for over 20 years.

I'm grateful to Georgia photographer and friend Richard Harrison, for all his magnificent photographs, and especially for the photo of my wood stove in Georgia, which appears on the back cover. Much winter writing took place by its fire. I miss it still.

I'm also grateful beyond measure to Dr. Clarissa Pinkola Estes, for her magnificent opus, *WOMEN WHO RUN WITH THE WOLVES.* It became my second bible for ten years. I still consult it regularly. Dr. Estes' gifts as storyteller, Jungian analyst and scholar of intercultural studies have enabled women to reconnect with those fierce, healthy, visionary and creative aspects of our deep instinctual nature. This nature, which she identified as the *'Wild Woman Archetype',* exists in all women. We find ourselves on every page and our souls leap up in delight.

Finally, I am grateful to all those participants who have come to Sacred Journal workshops to bravely engage in the deepening work of self discovery and spiritual growth. I know from personal experience, that God loves wild hearted women who don't always toe the line, and so many of you have graced my life. Thank you!

Table of Contents

On Using This Book 1
How All This Happened................................. 3
A Wild Hearted Inner Child............................ 11
Humility... 19
Patience... 35
Humor... 51
Love.. 67
Creativity... 81
Discernment... 97
Receptivity to Truth 113
Trust 129
Faith... 147
Gratitude 163
Grace 179
Wisdom... 195
Additional Food for the Wildish Soul 210
Acceptance.. 213
Papa's Love Letter..................................... 217
Resources for Tending the Soul Garden......... 225
About the Author 233

On Using This Book

The creation of this book came out of writing in my own journal, and conducting numerous workshops in what I now call the Sacred Journal Process. It is said that we always teach what we ourselves most need to learn. That's eminently true in my case. I learn this stuff more deeply and in new ways, every time I facilitate a workshop, guide a yoga class or revisit what I've written here.

The uses of a personal journal are many. Putting the pen to the page is a powerful process for accessing inner wisdom, inner truth, and discovering what you really think, want, fear, and hope. That's only for starters. If you're not already aware of the value of sacred journaling, I encourage you to sample it in this book.

For this reason, each of the disciples introduced here are followed by a series of Sacred Journal Questions, to help till up the soil of your feminine soul and invite fresh light into the garden of your life. A few blank pages follow the questions, for your personal responses. Write whatever comes! Let the heart speak. Put down the first thoughts that leap into your mind. These contain sprouts of fresh, wild truth; soul truth that may not have yet been discovered, or admitted to awareness for various reasons. Yet within these first thoughts are the juices of creativity, wisdom, and guidance for the direction and deepening of your life. You have it all within, and more where that came from. Yet life can spin and shred us like salad greens, by sending us in too many directions to access it. The personal journal is a method of entering the river of living wisdom that flows through each one of us. You can use this book and these questions to gently step into that water. See what happens.

Finally, you are invited to discover your own Twelve Disciples, or however many you need to nourish your spiritual life and keep you sane enough to navigate in this crazy, upside-down world.

How All This Happened

It didn't happen overnight, I'll tell you that much.

While I've had a personal relationship with Jesus Christ for 40 years, it never occurred to me that I might benefit from developing my own twelve disciples.

Our relationship might be different from some you've heard about from other Christians. I hadn't asked Him to come into my heart or anything like that. In fact, when it all began, I was disgusted with church, disillusioned with Christianity, and contemplating a second divorce. It's a good thing Jesus has a lot of patience. Getting me 'halter trained' and willing to be led, hasn't been easy for either one of us!

It was the mid 70's, when the frontiers of psychology and Eastern spirituality were burgeoning with discovery about the mind-body connection, and the role of stress in health and disease. I soaked that up, doing what I could to apply it in my own life and the lives of people who came for help with their stress related disorders. With an undergraduate degree in psychology and a newly minted Master's in nursing, I was passionately interested in what helped people heal. I wanted church to be a place folks could come to heal body, mind and spirit, as well as worship. At that time, what I saw consisted of coffee hours, committee meetings, gossip, and a whole bunch of mask making. Honest exchange was rare, yet something kept me coming back. Maybe it was a ragged thread of hope that I'd find what others had apparently found that kept *them* coming back. Meanwhile, the gnawing hunger for spiritual sustenance that felt psychologically healthy, beckoned me beyond church. That expedition included Hatha Yoga, Theosophy, the Edgar Cayce teachings, and learning to meditate. It was the best recipe I could have encountered then. The Holy Spirit leads us down many pathways they don't tell you about at church.

For months I'd been meditating, mostly without feeling much of anything other than wondering if 20 minutes had passed. Then one winter day, during a period of intense stress in both marriage and church, I explored a guided meditation. It focused on finding one's inner healer. Though I'd had training in clinical uses of guided imagery and various methods of meditation, I'd not explored this particular exercise. After reading through the instructions, I closed my eyes and started through the steps with no idea what to expect. When I came to the place where the 'inner healer' was to appear, I was dumb struck!

Jesus himself showed up, a smile on his face, looking like a blend of modern hippie and somebody's big brother.

"You didn't expect me, did you . . ." He offered gently.

Tears stung and spilled down my cheeks as I felt His presence fill the room.

"You are one of Mine" He continued, *"but there are three things you need to remember:"Don't confuse Christianity with church. Don't confuse Christ with Christianity. And don't confuse your direct experience of Me with anything anyone tries to teach you about Me. You come to Me directly . . . Okay?"* Then he disappeared, leaving me in a puddle of sobs.

I had been spoken to, my heart-mind pierced. In that moment I knew I belonged to Him, no matter what. I didn't fully understand what He told me then, but His words were branded into my memory. Like a lot of Truth that eventually frees us, its meaning evolves and deepens as we evolve and open.

I got over expecting church to take the place of coming to Him - and making space for Him to come to me – during meditation and in my journal. It would be 20 years before I'd learn the metaphysical significance of His twelve disciples. During those ensuing years Jesus never kept me from exploring the treasures of other traditions. He's accompanied me into Native American sweat lodges, women's' drumming circles, a Buddhist meditation retreat, and numerous 'Wild Woman' gatherings.

Through it all, traditional mainstream church has continued to anchor and nourish me. It still does today. I don't always resonate with everything spoken from the pulpit, or what happens within the congregation. We're all human beings, with shortcomings, limited perceptions and strong opinions, as well as goodness, gifts, generosity and strengths. I still need to sing the hymns, hear sermons, and excavate the historical tradition of my spiritual roots. There are timeless treasures and truths in Biblical scripture that expand my heart and open my mind. The difference is, I'm no longer confined to historical versions of Jesus taught in church. For me He's alive and willing to relate to any of us who make inner room for Him.

It wasn't until 1989, at a splendid little Unity church in Gainesville, Georgia, that the seeds for this manuscript were planted.

I'd moved there a year earlier, and began attending a gorgeous United Presbyterian church, with a magnificent organ and large choir. I loved the sermons. One Sunday, amid a collective gasp, the minister announced his resignation. I then learned there was a huge split in the church. I'd been through two of those before, and hadn't the stomach for another. Someone at work suggested I try the Unity church.

I'd never been exposed to Unity, much less the metaphysical dimension of Christianity. On learning what they taught; discovering how friendly they were to other denominations and traditions, this seemed more like what Jesus would do. It was chicken soup for my hungry soul. I quickly felt at home.

We were then a gathering of about 30 that met in a store front building that formerly housed a gun shop. The congregation included Quakers, folks who called themselves 'recovering Catholics', Methodists or Baptists, and others undergoing various life changes. Sunday services included a period of lovely meditation. So did Wednesday evenings. We didn't have a full time minister then and nobody seemed to mind.

One Sunday, a Unity minister from Atlanta spoke about Seth, the third son of Adam and Eve. I'd never heard of Seth! The unvarnished truth is, I'd not really studied the Bible either. She pointed out that after Cain and Abel, Seth (whose name means 'the settled one'), made possible the continued evolution of humanity. Afterward, I asked where I could learn more about what she taught us. "Do you have The Unity Metaphysical Bible Dictionary?" she asked. I didn't know there was such a thing. "I'm sure your bookstore has it," she replied, walking with me precisely to where it was. I promptly purchased one.

In addition to their Greek and Hebrew meanings, I learned each name and city in the Bible has a metaphysical meaning - which symbolically relates to human spiritual development! The Bible suddenly came alive in a way that interfaced with everything I'd learned in spiritual psychology, quantum physics, and the whole mind-body connection.

Shortly after, my friend Jamie lent me her copy of *The Twelve Powers of Man* by Charles Fillmore. Fillmore was the co-founder of the Unity movement over a hundred years ago. Unity teaches that the Twelve Powers refer to 12 spiritual energy centers in the subconscious of man. Fillmore's theory specifically locates each one in the human body and brain. According to Unity theory, these powers are Faith, Love, Strength, Wisdom, Power, Imagination, Understanding, Will, Order, Zeal, Elimination and Life. They are human expressions of the Christ nature contained within each of us. The word 'disciple' is derived from the root word, 'discipline'. These 12 powers, according to Fillmore, represent the Twelve Disciples Jesus called to follow Him, to carry out His mission. Peter represents Faith. John symbolizes Love, Bartholomew, imagination, etc. In Hebrew, the name Jesus, means 'I am.'

When something rings true in your cells, you know how your soul leaps up 'Yes! Yes! Yes!'? Well that's what happened to me. I devoured that little book. I highlighted, underlined and made so many notes in the margins I had to buy Jamie a new copy.

Fillmore's theory is something akin to the twelve meridian pathways of traditional Chinese medicine (on which acupuncture is based). It also resonated with what I already knew of the seven vital energy centers (chakras) discovered by yoga practitioners five thousand years earlier. By the early 1980's technology had recorded the light frequencies and subtle sounds of the chakras. I'd heard a recording of them myself.

At this time, I was deep into mid-life change, learning more about who I was and was not. What I'd learned about being a woman in our masculine dominated culture and church was up for squinty-eyed re-evaluation. So was the health care system I saw. My identity as a nurse was dissolving and scaring the bejeebers out of my ego. How would I make a livelihood? What about the bills? Who am I now? Where am I going? What IN THE WORLD is happening to me?

Jesus was always there, often with quiet humor that cracked me up. I questioned Him mercilessly. I argued with Him. He always won. It's like He'd give my mental kaleidoscope a quarter turn. Everything would fall into a new pattern – even if it's all the same stuff. That still happens.

Amid all this, I began to contemplate my own twelve disciples. Did they *have* to be the same as those of Charles Fillmore? After all, he was a *man*, living a century earlier. I was a *woman*, living now! I might need to develop different spiritual disciplines. One morning at my picnic table (where I loved to breakfast, meditate and write in my journal), I asked myself, What are the disciplines *I* need to develop to become whatever God wants *me* to be next? Faith and Love for sure, but what else? I already had way too much judgment, and plenty of imagination. I hadn't a clue. But I can tell you this: If you ask Jesus to join you, and wait in silence with an open heart, you *will* get a response.

In less than five minutes all 12 flowed out on the page - Love, Trust, Creativity, Faith, Discernment, Patience, Gratitude, Humility, Wisdom, Receptivity-to-Truth (a big one for me), Humor and Grace. I wrote them down as they came. Each day after, I meditated on them, breathing in the feeling of each one several times, before moving on to the next. They became *my* Twelve Disciples. Whenever I had a problem, I'd walk it through them. That simple process would invariably transform my way of seeing the situation. If my ego was having a hissy fit about something, Jesus would suggest we call a 'committee meeting'. He'd come too, if I needed a mediator. To stay focused I usually did that work in my journal. Yet sometimes all I needed was to consult briefly with Patience, Humility or Discernment. That I could do in my imagination.

Around this time my dear friend Barbara visited from Illinois, gifting me with a copy of Dr. Clarissa Pinkola Estes' landmark book, *Women Who Run with the Wolves* (New York, Ballantine Books, 1992). That book changed my life and continues to do so, each time I pick it up. Back then, it was mother's milk for my wildish feminine soul, enabling the left wing, maverick Christian I am, to stand on her feet, find her voice and take her place in my life. (More about this book in the *Additional Food for the Wildish Soul* section, on p. 225)

There are other 'disciples' I often need in my life, such as Forgiveness, Peace and Courage. However, my original 12 usually lead me straight to them anyway. So I've kept the ones given me that morning, now years ago.

It was DoitMyway, my lively inner child who suggested bringing these 'disciples' to life on the page the way you find them here. We had fun doing that together. I learned a lot too. In fact, DoitMyway has helped me so much, that I crowned her the first disciple of all. I realize that makes thirteen, but it's okay. In *Women Who Run with the Wolves*, Dr. Clarissa Pinkola Estes writes that while the number twelve represents completion, thirteen represents a new beginning.

May it be so for you . . .

*"What I tell you in the darkness
speak in the light;
and what you hear whispered in your ear,
proclaim on the housetops."*

- Jesus (Matthew 10:27)

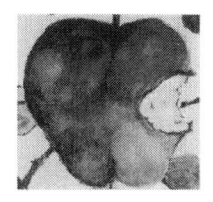

A Wild Hearted Inner Child

Her name is DoitMyway, that child I once was and left behind to join what she calls the world of 'adultery'. According to DoitMyway, adultery is a disease of civilization, characterized by 'should – ing' on yourself in public as well as at home. This is accompanied by advanced stages of people pleasing, high levels of unnecessary guilt and dangerously low serum fun levels. People who become completely adulterated typically lose their front truth in early childhood and some never get it back. They tend to develop hardening of the attitudes early in life and by age 45, may have no sign left of a living inner child.

DoitMyway knows how to make fun out of the most dull and dreary tasks - and escape altogether, from those that drag on too long. A lively mix of wise innocence, tender sensitivity, bravery and smart aleck outspokenness, this collection would not exist without her. She was re-introduced to me at a weekend workshop in the North Georgia Mountains. I was in my early 50's - ripe time for this sort of reclamation.

I'd moved to Georgia to take a position that promised to be the greatest move in my professional nursing career. It quickly morphed into a nightmare that would squeeze and wring the life force dry. However, I firmly believe there are no accidents. When Humpty Dumpty falls from the wall and nothing will put him together again, it's because that 'egg' needed to crack open! An unknown life, developing inside is readying for birth. That would prove true for me. eventually, but the first two years were hard.

Alone in a new part of the country, in the job from hell, I also had a next door landlady who, when she learned I taught yoga, decided I might be of the devil. She alternated between offering to let me out of my lease and trying to save my soul by taking me to the huge Baptist church she attended. I patiently stood my ground. When I didn't sprout horns or a tail, she relaxed. Gathering the ragged shards of my ego, I looked around for what might restore a measure of sanity. Yoga does that for me, so I offered a class through the local park and recreation department. To my delight, people came! In the weeks following, I met people who would open doors and accompany me through the next amazing chapter of my life.

During this time, I embarked on a Fourth Step Inventory. The Fourth Step is part of the Twelve Steps to Recovery originally used in Alcoholics Anonymous. I don't consider myself an alcoholic, but my father, an uncle and an especially beloved aunt on my mother's side, had all died in their disease. Besides being an A.C.O.A. (adult child of an alcoholic family), I had all the identified traits of an eldest child. We love to be in control, mostly because while growing up, chaos was the order of the day. We can adapt to almost any situation for a time, but don't always set healthy boundaries. We function well in emergencies, but may not know how to relax and go with the flow of things. We're great givers but resistant receivers, especially when it comes to asking for and receiving help. Maybe this 'searching and fearless moral inventory' would help me discover why life had taken this weird turn.

So, I purchased a Twelve-Steps-for-Everyone workbook, and set about my Fourth Step Inventory under the guidance of a wise old Apache Elder named Gray Hawk. Gray Hawk was a former alcoholism counselor who still loved helping "those who want to help themselves." I'd long been interested in Native American spirituality. It seemed like a good fit. Besides, he vaguely reminded me of my deceased father, whom I'd not yet fully forgiven for being such a mess.

Unbeknownst to me, DoitMyway was already at work under cover - along with Jesus. I'd later learn the two often work as a team.

After two months of excavating my character defects on paper and meeting weekly with Gray Hawk, I began to wonder if the Fourth Step ever ended. Gray Hawk assured me it was NOT to be hurried through. I continued plugging away. To further shore up my sanity (since I'd not yet departed the job from hell), I joined a creative writing class held at the Unity church. Taught by Linda (one of the first to join my yoga class), we were encouraged to get loose in the water, write from the heart and be outrageous! That was all it took to get DoitMyway in the game.

From around some hidden corner in my adulterated mind, she threw out an idea I couldn't ignore. Why not create characters out of my character defects? Yeah, give 'em names! Let them tell their story. Who knows? Maybe they serve a purpose! The counselor inside me leaped on the bait. Soon the *"One-eyed, One Armed Flying Purple People Pleaser, the Awfulizer* (an olympic broad jumper, who can leap to the worst possible conclusions in a New York minute), came to life on the page, along with *What'lltheythink and the Truth Fairy.*

The following week I shared two of them in the writing class. "I've got one of those in me!" several exclaimed. I sensed was on to something. My Fourth Step took on energy – until I shared my discovery with Gray Hawk.

His response was glowering disapproval. "The Fourth Step is NOT supposed to be FUN!" he growled. "It's meant to be a searching and fearless MORAL inventory!" Silently holding my ground, I felt my inner ears flatten, my hackles rise. Something inside vehemently whispered, 'It also doesn't HAVE to be FUNLESS!' (That was probably DoitMyway). Respecting what he had to say, I thanked Gray Hawk for his time, all the while sensing I'd likely not be back anytime soon.

I didn't know waiting in the wings was the new 'sponsor' for my Fourth Step - and the Fifth as well. Linda, the creative writing instructor, was certified in recovery counseling as well as journalism. She would also become a life-long friend.

Dr. Art and Kathy Powell were skilled counselors, who had become friends. When they announced a weekend intensive for *Getting in Touch With Your Inner Child*, I signed up. We gathered one Friday evening at the Center for New Beginnings in Dahlonega, GA. It was there, during a guided meditation, that I actually met DoitMyway.

Walking an imaginary beach, I saw a solitary little girl, her back to me, playing with a sand bucket and shovel. She looked to be around five with curly reddish hair. I watched from a distance a few moments before slowly approaching. As I drew nearer, another figure appeared from up the beach, walking toward her. It was Jesus. He reached her before I did. On seeing him, she leaped up, ran to Him and reached for His hand. Then turning, she saw me. Hanging on to Jesus, she sized me up.

"She belongs to you," Jesus offered gently as, still several feet apart, we faced each other. Tears welled in my eyes. "She's waiting for you to speak to her," Jesus said.

Unable to speak, I mutely held out my arms. She flew into them sobbing. . . . ."I've (sniff) waited for you all (sniff) this time" she hiccupped. . . . "You just left me (sniff) behind, like I didn't matter, and went off to join that awful world of adultery where there was no fun at all."

After a tearful reunion with lots of apologizing on my part, she snuffled awhile longer, then regained herself and stood up between Jesus and me.

What shall I call you? I asked.

"My name's DoitMyway," she announced firmly. "And I live real close to Him," she added, nodding up at Jesus.

"She named herself," He said, "but I capitalized the 'M' right away. This way there's no question as to WHOSE way is to be followed. She's pretty strong spirited, you know."

(I remembered that.) How shall I relate to her?

"By staying close to Me!" He laughed. "That's the idea! We both know what's best for you. DoitMyway will add some fun and creativity to the mix."

"But Mom," she interrupted, "you gotta promise *never* to leave me again! And for Heaven's sake, don't go back to that world of adultery unless you take me with you. Otherwise you'll get old before your time and dry up like an old apple!" I promised.

After that weekend, my writing life took off. So did opportunities to conduct seminars based on the rich stories in Estes's *Women Who Run With the Wolves*. By this time I was conducting yoga classes in three churches, and had a thriving practice in massage therapy. DoitMyway opened me to fresh adventures, on the page and off. She's at times outrageously outspoken and refuses to take life very seriously for very long. I never know what she'll suggest next. But I can count on it be creative, fun to consider, and notably truthful - *if* not always practical. I usually check it out with Jesus, who may have a slightly different angle from that of DoitMyway.

I began to write from the depths of my feminine mid-life change, which was rapidly morphing into a spiritual initiation. Essays on, *Disillusionment, Depression, Resilience & Rebirth*, and living on a *'Lilies of the Field Financial Plan'* formed into a collection entitled *Weeds & Wildflowers* –*Tales from the Wilderness of a Feminine Mid-life Change* (the next publishing adventure!).

(A third collection, *Life in the Soul Lane* is emerging from the garden of my life as an Elder woman. It will hopefully take its place too, in the unfolding scheme of soulful creation).

*"Then your light shall break forth like the dawn,
and your healing shall spring up quickly."*

- Isaiah 58:6

*The old is gone, the new is here,
And I am becoming increasingly clear.
Out of what I am and what I am not,
Something new is occurring,
I can't yet tell what!*

- DoitMyway

HUMILITY

"Going into the forest requires us to let go of our old ways and identities; we shed defenses, ingrained habits and attitudes, which opens us up to new possibilities and depth."

- Jean Shinoda Bolen
CROSSING into AVALON

Humility

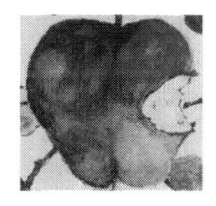

When I first met Humility, it was through DoitMyway. She said he was her best friend, along with Truth, Love and Humor. If I were willing to get out of my adulterated, rational mind and go on an adventure, she'd take me to meet him.

"Humility is as old as time itself," she informed me. "I realize you haven't met him yet, but I think it's time. There's nothing to fear. You'll like him. He's really friendly." Having no clue what I'd encounter, I agreed to go. In a serious manner, she told me to close my eyes, open my heart and take her hand. I did. As my imagination opened, this wild-hearted child led me along a path into a forest of fragrant old trees. Presently we came to a clearing, from where I saw in the distance, a grand old southern mansion, not far from the sea.

"That's where we're going, Mom. It's where he lives."

Skeptical that such a grand place would be home to Humility, I queried, "You sure?"

"Yup, don't you recognize it? You live there too!"

"Me!? I've never seen this place before . . ." Instantly I knew that wasn't true. I had been there before, years ago, as an undergraduate psychology student. It was 1970. We were in a mini-term on Transpersonal Psychology. In a guided meditation, we were invited to find an imaginary dwelling place, where all the various parts of our personality lived together. It was this same old southern mansion that appeared to me then, though I'd never visited the South. Now it beckoned me again, this time at the hand of my inner child.

We approached an entry way that looked like a leftover from *Gone with the Wind.* With authority, DoitMyway knocked on the door. I waited, a little uneasy. The door was opened - by Humility himself. A huge African American in elegant servant livery, his presence was powerful and warm. On seeing DoitMyway, his face broke in a wide grin as he opened his arms. She leaped into them and he picked her up, laughing. My eyes filled as they clung to each other in a bond that existed before time.

Putting her down, he resumed a dignified demeanor, bowing slightly to me. "Welcome" he said, in a baritone that sounded like the voice of James Earl Jones. "Your visit is much anticipated." We were ushered inside.

DoitMyway, obviously at home in this place, quickly disappeared, leaving me alone with Humility.

"This place has many rooms," he said in that cello voice, "and they all belong to you."

He went on to explain this was the mansion of my own deep psyche; that he too, was part of that. He hoped I'd make myself at home here. He'd do anything he could to be of service.

I asked how long he had lived here.

"Forever," he replied respectfully. "I come from a long line of the Creator's servants. I was assigned to you from the beginning."

What was in all these various rooms? I wanted to know. He replied they each contained some part of myself, or my life, that I had shut away, or had not yet encountered. I could visit any room I chose, whenever I wanted. If I found any of them locked, to let him know. He had the keys to them all. He'd be glad to accompany me if I wished, to help me become re-acquainted. Then he excused himself and left of the room.

Looking around, I noticed a long corridor with rooms on either side, like I faintly remembered from years ago. Then I noticed something else: a spiral staircase leading to a second, third and fourth level - and another leading downward to a deeper, underground level. A chill crept up my spine. I wasn't sure I wanted to know what was there. A feeling of lonely uneasiness wrapped around my shoulders when Humility reappeared, accompanied by DoitMyway. They carried trays of tea and cookies.

"This is a pretty cool place, don't you think Mom? Humility's pretty neat too, huh?"

Handing me tea in an exquisite china cup, Humility smiled. "She's the one that's neat" he said. "She's been a'wantin' you to come here a long time. We that live here, all of us been waitin'. Welcome home."

More tears sprang to my eyes. Lowering them, I sipped the tea. I'd entered the world of my own deep psyche. It had taken my brave little inner child to show it to me. Is this what Jesus meant when He said "and a little child shall lead them."?

Abruptly DoitMyway announced that we'd be going. "This is enough for now, Mom. You did really, really well." She took my tea and placed it on the tray. We bid Humility good-bye. He nodded, eyes smiling. "Now you know where you really live, and how to get here. It's an inside job." I heard myself promise to return. (Little did I know how often that would be.)

Outside, DoitMyway led us back to the path through the forest to the outer world my mind usually inhabited. "I just wanted you to know where this other place is" she said nonchalantly. "Besides, it was time for you to meet Humility. He'll be helpful in the time ahead. Now, I'm gonna go play. See ya later." With that she left.

Working on my Fourth Step Inventory in the months ahead, I returned to that mansion many times. Particularly when I came to another uncomfortable part of myself, or a memory snarled in a pocket of pain. Each time, Humility welcomed me offering refreshment and comfort. When I was ready, he'd silently accompany me to whatever chamber I needed to visit and unlock the door. Then he'd gently ask if I'd like him to stay with me. Sometimes I did.

With the help of Humility, DoitMyway and the Holy Spirit, my Fourth Step Inventory took on a sense of inner adventure, as well as healing. I discovered dimensions of myself that had never before had a voice.

*"Let not your heart be troubled.
Let it be surprised!"*

Jesus (to me)

*Behold, thou doest desire truth
in the innermost being;
and in the hidden part,
thou wilt make me know wisdom"*

- Psalm 51:6

Sacred Journal Questions from Humility

1. Let your inner child take you by the hand, bring you a cup of tea, and tell you what she wants you to know.

2. Allow the goddess within you to introduce herself. What does she want? What does she love? What advice does she have for you? What gift? (Be sure to give her a name.)

3. What do you need to release in order to have more life? What do you need to cultivate? What are you willing to do about that? If not now, when?

4. What matters most?

Notes

Notes

Notes

Notes

Notes

Notes

Notes

Notes

PATIENCE

"Do you realize that four out of every five Americans have a serious wait problem? That's right. Studies show that most Americans can't stand waiting. (They can't even SIT waiting.) Wait problems are being blamed for everything from heart disease to digestive disorders, high blood pressure to low income. . . . Actually it's not the wait itself that's harmful, but your attitude about your wait. Whenever people say to me, I hate to wait! I tell them they have things backward. They should wait to hate instead.

Yes, we are a society obsessed with speed. We live life by the clock. The second hand was invented about 300 years ago, and most of us have led a second-hand existence ever since. We are so concerned with what time it is, we forget that it is always now."

-from Steve Bhaerman's
DRIVING YOUR OWN KARMA
Swami Beyondananda's Tour Guide to Enlightenment.

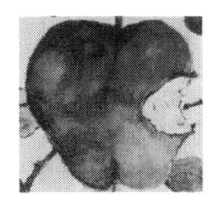

Patience

Patience was escorted into my private sanctuary by Humility. Neither of them was on my agenda that day. However, Humility advised me that Patience was gravely ill and requesting reassignment. It seems he's not thrived in my kingdom for years. According to Humility, he was too noble to come forth. Being what he is, he was accustomed to waiting. Just not this long I suppose.

When he entered I was shocked by his condition. His elegant field officer's uniform hung on his emaciated frame. The expression on his pale face was one of quiet nobility, his silently born distress too obvious to hide. I was exquisitely uncomfortable. This suffering servant apparently belonged to ME!

"Sit down," I said, gesturing to a chair in front of my queenly desk. With labored breath and as much dignity as his condition allowed, he sat, his eyes lowered. He appeared as uncomfortable with this meeting as I. "Tell me about yourself. I see you are not well. How can I help?"

"Well, Your Majesty," he began, clearing his throat and coughing, "I realize how busy you are. I don't want to take up your time. Perhaps it would be easiest if you simply honored my request to be reassigned. I brought an official transfer request with me. If you'll just sign it, that would take care of everything."

"Wait. Reassignment? Why? Have you not been treated well in my service? Have you not received whatever you needed?"

"Not exactly, Your Majesty" he replied hesitantly. "What I need has been the same since the Creator first assigned me to you"

"And what is that?" I'm now wincing at what the answer might be.

"It is not much actually. . . . I don't mean to be difficult or demanding. All I need is recognition, and an assignment as to where you want me to serve. Among all the disciples assigned to you, the others meet with you frequently. You consult with them. You give them work to do. Even Trust and Gratitude, who were also not utilized at first, now have their places in your life. I suffer from a profound case of uselessness which has seriously affected my center of inspiration. . . ." Abruptly he was seized by such a fit of coughing and wheezing that his lips turned blue and his face crimson.

Oh my god! I thought. Patience is what's been missing in me all this time! Now he's nearly dead from lack of use! Come to think of it, I don't remember ever requesting him . . . !

As if reading my thoughts, he gently interrupted. "That's true Your Majesty, you didn't ask for me. I was SENT to you, by direct orders from the Creator. I was advised I'd be greatly needed in the coming civil war between your ego and your Soul; that I'd have one of the most challenging assignments of my life. The Creator was concerned I'd be so overworked I might succumb to battle fatigue. But I reassured Him I loved nothing better than negotiating peace settlements. That's when I truly thrive! You see, if I'm not used I weaken and wither until . . . Well, you see how I am"

I did see! He looked downright fragile. This was all my fault! I had to make some sort of restitution to him - and maybe to the Creator as well. "What would it take for you to remain with me?" I asked. Patience considered this for long moments, twisting his hat in his hand. I waited while silence stretched between us.

Humility, who accompanied him, had remained respectfully at the far corner of the room. Now he gestured, asking whether he might join the discussion. I motioned him to sit in the chair next to Patience, which he did. "Tell her what you need" he said, nudging Patience. "Tell her like you told me"

Patience looked up slowly."I want a place in your life," he said. "I want to be of service. You see, I need to be regularly exercised or I'll die. I know that's not what the Creator intended when He sent me to serve you. On the other hand, I don't wish to be a burden."

Filled with remorse, I didn't want him to die - or leave. "Please stay" I pleaded, "and please forgive me. I've neglected you terribly. I've been blind. I feel awful. But why have you waited so long to come forth?"

"Well Your Majesty, with all due respect, I am what I am. I wait. Then I wait some more. It's my nature to accept whatever comes and whatever doesn't come. But when I was never called, and noticed I was seriously weakening, I thought perhaps I'd misunderstood my assignment. That was when Humility insisted I request this audience."

"I do want you to stay!" I repeated."I want to strengthen you, help you recover. What would best do that now?" More silence, more twisting his cap. Humility nudged him again."Tell her."

Patience raised his eyes to mine, his face flushing." I think if we just had some regular time together, Your Majesty, sort of like we're doing right now, that I'd be fit as a fiddle in no time. I'd be so honored for you to really get to know me. Maybe Humility could join us, at least at first, until I overcome my shyness and gain more strength."

"Is that all?" I asked incredulous. "Just time together?"

"Oh yes ma'am," he beamed, his eyes bright with the glint of a tear." That would do it all right. Could we meet again tomorrow? Or would that be too soon? I know how busy you are."

"Oh no," I replied, my own eyes moistening." Tomorrow would be just fine. In fact you could stay awhile right now if you'd like. I'll have some tea or coffee made. . . By the way, are you hungry?"

"Oh yes ma'am" he said longingly," I am. But I don't drink or eat the things you do. You've probably forgotten, but I'm not physical. I'm mostly spiritual and mental, with a few feelings and a handful of Soul thrown in."

"Of course! How silly of me. But . . . you said you were hungry. What then shall I give you?"

"My main food is recognition and respect. If you'd just spend a little time with me each day, I'd be in your service forever. I'd come when you call. I'd protect you from hasty decisions, and from the discouragement that comes when life doesn't happen like you hoped. I could also teach you how to let stories take their own time ripening, and guide you through the tedious task of reworking them. But for that, I'll have to recover my strength." Humility smiled, nodding. About that time, the door burst open and in skipped DoitMyway. On seeing Patience, she squealed with delight and flew to him, hugging his neck.

"You two know each other?" I asked, surprised.

"Sure we do!" she chirped, climbing on his lap."I betcha I know Patience a lot better 'n YOU do! Who do you think kept me company all those years while you were lost in the world of adultery? I nearly gave up and died, but Patience wouldn't let me. He said one of these days you'd come lookin' for me. Lately though, it's been *me* telling *him* not to give up. Wow! You two finally met! This is like a birthday party!"

And so it was. I canceled my agenda for the day, which included an interview for another 'real' job I didn't really want. We all went for ice cream and a walk in the park. DoitMyway made me promise to meet with Patience every day for the next month, and at least weekly thereafter. I suspect Humility put her up to that.

And I have led you these forty years in the wilderness;
your clothes have not worn out on you,
and your sandal has not worn out on your foot."

Your Papa
(Deuteronomy 29:5)

Sacred Journal Questions from Patience

1. What gift would PATIENCE give you, if you were willing to receive it?

2. What have you learned from PATIENCE, that you might not have learned any other way?

3. If you sat quietly with PATIENCE now, what would you learn? What else?

Notes

Notes

Notes

Notes

Notes

Notes

Notes

Notes

HUMOR

BEWARE OF OUGHTISM

"A lot of people say the problem with the world today is the Me Generation, where everyone is out doing what they want to do.

I say the real problem is the Who Me? Generation, which is people out doing what everyone ELSE wants them to do. And this condition, which I call Oughtism, is the disease of the oughtanomic nervous system where the unfortunate victims oughtamatically do what others tell them they ought to do. If left untreated, Oughtism can result in a total loss of the ability to think. Fortunately, there is an organization called S.T.O.P. – Society to Transcend Oughtistic Practices – which has made it their mission to end Oughtism on the planet by the year 2000. I'll tell you how pervasive this epidemic is. When people find out about the crusade to end Oughtism, the first thing they ask, What do you think I ought to do about it?"

- from Steve Bhaerman's
DRIVING YOUR OWN KARMA
Swami Beyondananda's Tour Guide to Enlightenment

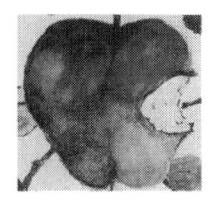

Humor

Humor is the Chief Security Guard in the Kingdom of Right Relationships. As soon as he was born, the Creator bestowed His blessing on this Holy Spirit child, and Humor grew in both wisdom and stature. The eldest son of Love and Laughter, his central task was to make sure thieves and robbers (such as fear, resentment, anxiety and prejudice) are identified, arrested and transformed before they do real damage. His second task was to entertain and lighten the heart. By the time he reached maturity, Humor had become a well known healer of mind, body, spirit and all sorts of relationships.

Tall, a little lanky, and lots of fun, Humor knows just where your funny bone is and he loves to tickle it - especially if he notices you're about to be seduced by Terminal Seriousness.

Terminal Seriousness seduces the vulnerable and unsuspecting into his dark spell of gloom, doom and fear (false evidence appearing real). These poisons promptly pollute the life force and weaken the capacity for joy and peace. Terminal Seriousness is terrified of Humor. He knows Humor can drop him in his tracks with a simple joke that sends gales of cleansing laughter through anyone he's managed to capture. Such was the case one day when I was seeing a new client.

It was just after 5:00 PM when the gentleman, appearing to be in his early 60's, arrived. He'd called the day before sounding somewhat urgent. Normally I had new clients fill out an in-depth stress inventory prior to a first appointment, which we'd discuss in that first session. There'd been no time for that.

As my previous client left, I found this fellow in the waiting room, head down, pacing back and forth. He didn't respond to my initial greeting. Continuing to pace, his eyes darted from the floor to me and back again. Most folks in the building have left by 5:00 PM. Aware I was alone on the third floor with this obviously disturbed chap, I tried to ignore the chilly knot tightening in my mid-section, urging me to open the door to the corridor - in the event I had to escape or yell for help. However, something stronger sat me down, insisting I simply breathe and wait.

Continuing to pace, he haltingly revealed why he'd come. He'd been seriously considering suicide. The thoughts were getting stronger. He'd never been to a 'shrink' before; never felt like he needed one. But nothing like this had ever happened to him. He didn't know what else to do. At least I was a nurse, not a 'shrink'.

It was the mid- 80's. The economy had nose-dived. A banker from a nearby community, he'd been forced to foreclose on a number of farm loans made to people he deeply cared about, families with whom he'd related for years. The pain had gotten too heavy to bear. Before this, he'd always loved his job. Now he hated going to work. But beneath that there was more, as is often the case, and more below that. Eventually he stopped pacing, slumped into a chair and buried his head in his hands.

The mood in the room had grown heavier and heavier. This man couldn't see any light at the end of his darkness. Listening to him, neither could I. He wanted out. I didn't blame him. He revealed that he'd begun to give away some of his things, including his business suits.

By this time, Humor and the Holy Spirit decided this attack by Terminal Seriousness had gone far enough. In the gloomy silence that followed his last sentence, I heard the words tumble out of my mouth, *Have you thought about what you're gonna wear at your funeral?*

My GOD! I couldn't believe I said that! The client sat upright, staring at me, shocked. I looked at him, equally shocked. My professional ego wanted to crawl in a hole. But the Holy Spirit knew better.

The client began to laugh a little. So did I - mostly from relief. Then he laughed some more, until he began to weep, and then to really weep in that deep, cleansing way that loosens the emotional dam that's been in place far too long. Humor and the Holy Spirit had saved the day, and maybe this man's life.

When he'd wept long and deeply enough for now, a peaceful silence filled the space between us. I invited him into the treatment room to get on the massage table fully clothed. With Jesus' guidance I did some gentle joggling of limbs and torso to loosen up his life-force, massaged his head and neck a little, and finished with hands on healing prayer. Before he departed, I arranged an appointment with a male psychologist for some testosterone-flavored talk therapy.

After that, Humor followed my professional work a little more closely. He still does, just to make sure I don't get too chummy with Terminal Seriousness.

Not long after moving to Georgia, God introduced me to '*Swami Beyondananda*' in a side splitting humor performance at the

Atlanta Unity Church. This brilliant 'brain child' and alter ego of writer/humorist Steve Bhaerman authored a hilarious little book, DRIVING YOUR OWN KARMA- Swami Beyondananda's Tour Guide to Enlightenment (Rochester, Vermont: Destiny Books, 1989).

A master at FUN-damentalism ("First the fun, then the mental"), it is obvious God poured out plenty of 'laugh force' on this fellow, and continues to do so. Check out his web-site! Laughter is after all, the best medicine – especially if you're in the pits.

"Life is a situation comedy that will never get cancelled, and if you listen carefully you will find that a laugh track has been provided."

- Swami Beyondananda

*Behold, I will pour out my spirit upon you.
I will make my words known to you . . ."*

- Proverbs 2:23

Sacred Journal Questions from Humor

1. When was the last time you couldn't NOT laugh, when you were expected to be deadly serious? Go ahead, cough it up. If it was back in grade school, you're way too chummy with Terminal Seriousness.

2. What's your serum fun level right this minute? What would raise it - for Heaven's sake? Write that down. Then - if it isn't illegal, doesn't harm anyone or get you put in jail – go do it- for Heaven's sake

3. What's that 'should' you're standing in? Did you do that all over yourself?

4. What are you doing to prevent TRUTH decay? You're the only one who can take care of your TRUTH. What does IT say?

Notes

Notes

Notes

Notes

Notes

Notes

Notes

Notes

LOVE

Love comes in many packages,
In people and places
You never expected.
Love tests you and tries you;
It shapes and defines you,
Until you eventually
Learn who you are,
And who God is,
And let go of the fear
Of it all.

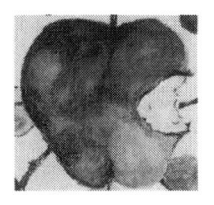

Love

Faced with the task of portraying Love as a Disciple, I feel stymied. Love wears so many faces. Where do I begin? I could write of the Love I've personally known, a Love who knows me better than I know myself. But that would limit what is unlimited, what can never be confined to human definition. So I invited Love to speak.

"I am the primary energy of the Creator. I initiate everything into its rightful relationship with everything else. When any part of the Creation is out of balance, I am the restorer of harmony. I am the way through which the Creator relates to the Creation in all its manifestations. That includes you. Like the wind, you do not know where I come from, or where I go. Yet you can see, feel, and sometimes even smell my Presence. Yes, I said smell. Your very cells remember the scent of Clorox on your mother's hands."

That's so true! I'd never thought of smell experiences as Love. Yet to this day, if I whiff the scent of bleach on someone's hands, memories of mom's love flood through me, lumping in my throat with longing. The fragrances of hay, grain and horse dung still send delight coursing through memories of caring for my horse. Soup on the stove and freshly cut grass fills me with private joy. I've known my share of Love too, in ways we're more socialized to expect - parents, teachers, those who are kind to us, believe in us, who help us, even when we don't deserve it. I've known Love with husbands, lovers and other close friendships.

"You've also felt My Presence in relationships and circumstances you never expected, some you'd not dare put on this page. But I know them. Love is not confined to the places and patterns your religious and social indoctrinations have led you to believe. In fact, you've been roundly disappointed in some of those, am I right?"

I was caught off guard. Two memories floated up, still stinging with remnants of pain I thought was long forgotten.

"Good girl," whispers Love. "You can't heal what you don't feel. Cough up those memories. Let yourself feel them. Have compassion for yourself as you re-member them. Then together let's soak them in a bath of forgiveness. Forgiveness is to sore memories what warm Epsom Salts are to sore muscles. Forgiveness allows for transformation. Without it they'll stay stuck inside, below your awareness."

More than once when my ego had given up, Love quietly transformed a snarled relationship when I wasn't looking, then set it free to show up in fresh clothing. On such occasions, I'm humbled into evolution, often against my will.

I tend to take things way too seriously, flogging myself with blame, shame, and obsessing over personal responsibility for whatever happens. More than once, while I'm in some sort of stew, Love has sent someone out of the blue, who says or does just the right thing.

Awhile back, I was struggling to accomplish something (don't even remember what), that no matter what I did or how I tried, it just wasn't happening. I was stuck, frustrated and had myself all in a wad, when my friend Ginny called. On hearing my tale, Ginny quoted from Goethe:*"If the task is not within your power, it's not your task."* It had never occurred to me that maybe this wasn't my task! What a relief!

"That was me," whispered Love. "I also work undercover, but I'm really everywhere. Look around you; into the eyes of a dog, a child, someone you love, even someone you don't like! Look up through a bare tree in winter, at falling snow. Listen to a garden at night. Let the silence of your soul open the door to the voice of the Holy Spirit. You'll hear my words, sense my peace and know my grace. You'll remember once more, that you can trust me to guide you and care for those you love.

I am the Way, the Truth and the Life. I do come that you might have life and have it much more abundantly. Though you don't always recognize me, I find ways to reach you wherever you are."

> *"I will ask the Father and He will give you another helper,*
> *that He may be with you forever.*
> *That is the spirit of Truth, whom the world cannot receive,*
> *because it does not behold Him or know Him.*
> *But you know Him, because He resides in you."*
>
> *- Jesus (John 14:16 – 17)*

Sacred Journal Questions from Love

1. When have you felt most loved? Give yourself ten minutes to list all those that come to mind. If you need more time, TAKE IT! Then let yourself fully feel that LOVE, all throughout your being. Give thanks.

2. When have you found it most difficult to love yourself, another, or a particular situation? How did that wound you? What did it strengthen in you? What have you learned from it?

3. Let LOVE speak to you now, and tell you what it wants you to know. Let yourself be surprised. (You might need extra paper).

Notes

Notes

Notes

Notes

Notes

Notes

Notes

Notes

CREATIVITY

"For most of us, the idea that the creator encourages creativity is a radical thought. We tend to think, or at least to fear, that creative dreams are egotistical, something God wouldn't approve for us. After all, our creative artist is an inner youngster and prone to wildish thinking."

> *- Julia Cameron*
> THE ARTIST'S WAY

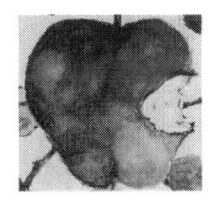

Creativity

Creativity loves colors, contrasts and collages of things that look really nice together. For as long as I can remember, she's been my Soul's closest playmate. On learning my ABC's, she chose colors for each letter of the alphabet, which I still carry today. Around that time, she also helped me commit my first crime.

Since I'd not yet learned to climb a whole flight of stairs alone, Mom kept the stairwell and basement doors in our farm house carefully locked. The winter of my brother's birth, an elderly woman named Mattie came to stay with us to help Mom. Mattie wore her gray hair in a bun, and made artificial flowers out of crepe paper in her upstairs room. Mom took me up there one day to see them. I didn't like Mattie much and I don't think she liked me. She got a lot crankier when Mom wasn't around. What makes my crime even more serious is that Mattie used crutches. One foot and ankle didn't work right, and sort of dragged. But neither Creativity nor I had developed much moral consciousness yet. We were content to explore and see how we could make stuff work.

One afternoon Mom went to town. I was supposed to be down for a nap. Mom said a nap would make time pass faster 'til she got home. I tried. I really did. While my baby brother slumbered in his crib, Mattie peeked in on us twice. Lying still, I kept my eyes almost shut, leaving the teensy, tiniest opening. Apparently satisfied, Mattie went upstairs to her room. Soon I heard her sewing machine. Exulting in a sense of freedom, Creativity and I crept out of bed, into the kitchen and set about exploring on tip toe.

In the dining room we discovered the door to upstairs left open! The dark stairwell, with its winding upward turn, promised adventure.

Creativity convinced me if we were careful how we went about it we could climb those stairs just fine. Silent as cotton, we slowly negotiated the ascent - on all fours - while Mattie's treadle sewing machine thumped away. Mom would be so happy to see I could climb stairs.

Upon reaching the summit, we found the door to Mattie's room closed. As her machine continued its happy racket, I contemplated surprising her with my latest feat. Maybe she'd let me watch her make flowers 'til Mom got home. But the priority of personal freedom overcame such an unlikely response on the part of Mattie. Besides I didn't like her that well. What to do next?

Creativity pointed to the hook and eye latch on Mattie's closed door. It was way too high for me to reach, but Creativity noticed a chair just inside the room across the hall. I knew how to pull up chairs to things when I needed them. Quietly we slid that chair into place. Mattie's machine never missed a stitch. Up I climbed, sank that hook in the eye, and got back down.
Our freedom assured, we next considered how to approach the descent.

Creativity suggested sitting on the top step and scooting on our bottom, one step at a time. It was great fun. It didn't make any noise, and thanks to my slumbering brother, Creativity and I had the house to ourselves!

I don't know what else we did that day, but I clearly remember Mom's startled look when she got home and saw me happily playing by myself. "Where's Mattie?" she asked nervously. About then, Mattie began frantically calling downstairs, that she was locked in. Mom hurried up the stairs, puzzled as to how such a thing could ever have happened. There she found the evidence of my crime: the chair left in place.

After that, Mom didn't leave me with Mattie. It had something to do with Mattie being hard of hearing. But Creativity and I were inseparable. We became expert at pushing the limits in ways that didn't involve further crime or cause more chaos than together we could handle.

Growing up, Creativity couldn't decide whether we should be a ballerina, a concert pianist, a lounge singer or a professional horsewoman. The only things we really liked in high school were art, music and creative writing. No one in my family had gone to college. At 17 I wasn't interested either. However, after a couple of office jobs, Destiny introduced me to Reason. His motives were respectable, and everyone hoped I would marry him. Within in a year of our relationship, I was transported from my enjoyable (occasionally boring) job as receptionist for a large manufacturing firm, into the conformity driven world of professional nursing school. People around me were relieved and encouraging. Now I'd have a reliable profession to "fall back on."

It was a laudable goal in my salt-of-the-earth Midwestern upbringing. I graduated at the top of my class and was on my way to becoming thoroughly adulterated.

Knowing I was not destined for the confines of institutional nursing or even academic life, Creativity allowed Reason to have his way with me awhile longer. She held on tight while I was schooled in ways that lit fires of understanding about human growth, development, physiology, psychology, health, disease and healing. I loved the learning. An undergraduate degree in psychology gave Creativity all the fuel needed to make her case for putting our professional life together in a new way. A Master's in nursing added teaching credentials and subsequently led to a creative private practice in wellness education. Eventually the caregiver I'd become gave birth to a creative writer.

The two co-existed for several years, with growing tension between Creativity and Reason. Finally, Creativity drew a line in the sand. The caregiver would have to take a back seat to the creative writer – permanently.

That unleashed a civil war between my Ego and Soul, requiring regular mediation by Jesus Christ, and heavy doses of Faith, Trust, Grace, Humility and Gratitude. During that war Creativity met and married Humor. The two gave birth to twin daughters, Whimsy and Serendipity. They visit whenever they know I'm working on a story, or if they happen to notice that my serum fun level has tanked.

The marriage of Creativity left Reason with a broken heart. For years, he'd secretly loved Creativity and hoped one day to marry her. When it became obvious that wasn't going to happen, Destiny helped Reason take his rightful place in my life. She assigned him the task of teaching me to compose on the computer. In this way we all finally found a mostly harmonious way of living together, which resulted in, among other things, this manuscript! I don't know what I'd do without Creativity. She says I don't have to worry about that.

*He leadeth me and knows the way which I know not.
And yet He would not keep me from all He would have me learn.
And so I trust Him to communicate to me,
all that He knows for me."*

- A Course in Miracles

*"For the Lord your God has blessed you
in all that you have done;
He has known your wanderings
through this great wilderness.
These forty years the Lord your God
has been with you; and you
have not lacked a thing."*

*-Your Papa
(Deuteronomy 2:7)*

Sacred Journal Questions from Creativity

1. Create an ideal day for yourself. Describe it in detail. Let yourself loose on the page. No one has to see it but you!

2. List all the ways you allow yourself to create. What, if anything, is missing?

3. What does your Soul have to say about that? What does your inner child suggest you do about it?

4. If your life were a novel, what would it's title be? Allow yourself to write a short synopsis and chapter outline. Which chapter are you currently living?

Notes

Notes

Notes

Notes

Notes

Notes

Notes

Notes

DISCERNMENT

"A woman's issues of soul cannot be treated by carving her into a more acceptable form as defined by an unconscious culture, nor can she be bent into a more intellectually acceptable shape by those who claim to be the sole bearers of consciousness."

- Clarissa Pinkola Este
WOMEN WHO RUN WITH THE WOLVES

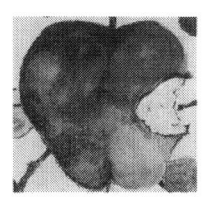

Discernment

Discernment is a spirit woman with three eyes in her head and one in her navel. The only daughter of Disillusionment, Discernment tends the fires of a woman's truest nature. The three eyes in her head are the eye of Owl for seeing in the dark, the eye of Raven to summon transformation, and the eye of Eagle to see the truth from a high place and far distance. The eye hidden in her navel is the eye of She-wolf. That eye is trained to discern which of our instincts are healthy, and which have become injured or anesthetized through over domestication.

She-wolf recognizes poison bait and leg traps. She may direct you to take a sudden U-turn or change your mind at the last moment, without knowing why.

With her eye of Owl, Discernment wakens a woman out of sleep in the hours past midnight. Across the dark silence, she calls . . . Whooo . . . Whooo . . . Whooo are you now? Whooo . . . are these in your life that scatter your energies . . . ? Whooo . . . is being served? . . . Whooo is being sacrificed?

In the night stillness, Owl permits you to find the answers cradled in the crescent moon, as you sit beside her, on the bare branches of your current situation.

The eye of Raven summons the medicines needed for transformation. She will turn tribulation, even tragedy, into fresh truth that illumines your path toward authentic freedom. Raven's eye determines the precise ritual or ceremony required for healing. She'll lead you into the dance of it, until you learn the dance for yourself. You must however, be willing to follow Raven's directions, even when they seem foolish, and those around you don't understand. Discernment knows what she's doing. I've learned to trust her Raven eye.

The eye of Eagle carries you to a place higher than your ordinary mind could go without her. From there you'll be able to glimpse the other side of the present mountain of doubt, devastation, depression or discouragement. From this high place, Eagle will help you see where all your fertile dreams and true gifts await your arrival to claim them. You'll receive her assurance that you are being safely guided and fully provided, in the likely case you have forgotten again.

So when Discernment knocks on your door (and of course she will), welcome her to your heart and hearth. She is a powerful and dedicated servant of your soul. While her appearance may be strange, and the hour she appears inconvenient, she has a message you likely need, maybe right at this moment. No true love can flourish without Discernment. No true forgiveness or lasting peace. Besides, without her four sacred eyes, you may never find the hidden treasures of your true Self.

Discernment first knocked on the door of my psyche in my mid- 40's. Women were beginning to tell the truth about their lives and their spirituality. We were collectively discovering that our personal truths didn't match what we were socialized to believe they would – if we were just sufficiently loving, compliant, virtuous and obedient. While I was well educated, enjoying private practice as a professional nurse, I was also naïve. I'd not yet encountered that 'wise-woman' inside me; that one who sees through superficial layers; the one with sufficient detachment to cut away that which doesn't serve me well.

It was late October. October is full of mystery and magic. During a week long conference on traditional Indian medicine for health care professionals, I met one of the presenters – a 'medicine man'. He invited me to dinner that evening. I was flattered. Over the next few weeks we came to know each other, superficially. I was temporarily smitten - until I learned he'd lied about his 'domestic' situation. The 'medicine' I would next need was about to be delivered – from inside - by Discernment herself.

That night I went to sleep troubled.

Before dawn, I was half wakened by the shadowy figure of a medieval woman in a hooded, black cloak, peering into the night through an iron gate. Holding a lamp in one hand and a sword in the other, she aimed her lamp toward a dark male figure on horseback approaching the gate.

"No false knights in the castle!" she hissed in a tone that stopped him in his tracks.

I sat upright, breathing in the scene, which remained in place for a time. From Jungian psychology, I knew that all parts of a dream are parts of the self, wanting to be known.

This shadowy woman was some part of me, a fierce, dark dimension I didn't know. Before she left, I learned her name was *Aphrodite*. I didn't go back to sleep. The morning light revealed a killer frost had destroyed the flowers lining my driveway. Such was my initiation into the hidden dimensions of my deeper psyche.

In Greek mythology, Aphrodite is the goddess of love and mother of Eros (relationship). I learned what I could about this archetypal goddess, and welcomed her to my inner world.

The best way I can describe *my* Aphrodite, is a cross between Rosalind Russell's *Auntie Mame* and *Cruella DeVille*. I would need her lamp, her sword and her wonderful humor, as I dealt with that 'medicine man' and more of my own naïve illusions about seductive relationships.

So yes, I 'hear' voices. And they're all mine! Discernment helps determine which of them is serving me well.

Sacred Journal Questions from Discernment

1. So, whooo are you now? How are you different than last year at this time? Than five years ago?

2. What can you now see, perhaps from your past - or in the present - with new eyes?

3. When have you had to tolerate ambiguity, or hold the tension of two opposing possibilities, until you reached clarity with confidence?

4. What in your recent or present life now needs to be held up for squinty-eyed re-evaluation?

Notes

Notes

Notes

Notes

Notes

Notes

Notes

Notes

Notes

RECEPTIVITY To TRUTH

The Truth will set you free.
But first it might make you miserable!

-Unknown

The Truth about Truth Decay – Yes, There is a Cure

"It is sad indeed to watch so many people develop cavities in truth after truth until they haven't a truth left in their heads – especially when caring for your truth is so simple. Want to prevent truth decay? Then use mental floss every day. Mental floss is invisible, but you CAN feel it. Draw one end of the floss into your right ear, and listen it through to the middle of your brain until it comes out the other side. If you listen as well as most people, you should have no problem having something go in one ear and out the other. Now then, gently move the floss back and forth, and as you do so, you will feel hardened ideas and putrefying thoughts dislodge. Do this twice a day and you will feel a remarkable clarity. Before long, you will be in constant touch with Divine Truth: God is Divine, and we are the fruit of the Divine, destined for grapeness."

-from Steve Bhaerman's
DRIVING YOUR OWN KARMA
Swami Beyondananda's Tour Guide to
Enlightenment

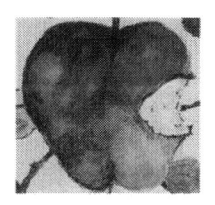

Receptivity to Truth

In her early development, Receptivity was willing to receive whatever came her way. Unless accompanied by Truth however, she was in danger of succumbing to spiritual predators and parasites that can derail human life and drain its vital energies. Only after undergoing a lengthy internship with Discernment, was Receptivity wise enough to recognize and welcome the Spirit of Truth - which admittedly can upset the order of ordinary life. Upon completion of her studies with Discernment, Receptivity received her full name.

Now Receptivity to Truth is a seasoned Disciple, with a gift for discriminating between what is true and what is not. (I sometimes call her my bull-shit detector).

Receptivity has another gift which enables one to release limited ways of thinking. She knows how to create open spaces in the psyche, where none existed before. If I sit in silence and summon her help, she'll draw an imaginary door on some solid wall of my limited thinking. Then, if I'll remain there in silence, she'll open that door. On the other side is a lovely space filled with light. She'll invite me to enter. I don't always want to go. It's easier to remain in the rational rooms of my mind, with my carefully constructed beliefs and protective perceptions held firmly in place. Aware that entering the Unknown is the key to expanded life, Receptivity waits.

Contemplating that empty space, I query "What's in there"?

"Nothing" she replies, *"until you get here. If you decide to enter, you'll have to wait awhile in the light, bringing only the true desires of your heart. Everything else must be left behind, including your fears and usual ways of thinking. Stop filling your time and your mind with that which is unrelated to your true desires. Those contain the keys to your expansion. Lay down your burdens, focus on those and come through this door. I'll be with you."* I finally relent and enter.

Together we rest in that light, allowing my dreams and heart's desires to have center stage. Imagining how it would feel to be living them, I try to remain open to whatever Heaven sends in the way of guidance. I've never actually seen her, yet those who have, say Truth rides a magnificent horse, with wings on its feet and a flowing mane. They say she'll reach down to lift the veil from whatever illusion it's time to release. Then giving her blessing, she rides off into the mists. When she visits me, Truth sometimes brings hope and joy. Other times however, she brings sadness, pain, grief or disappointment. It's those painful visits of Truth that seem to remain with me longer. Humility says that's because I haven't yet fully forgiven whatever it was, including myself.

In those times of pain or drama, Jesus has been known to drop by, completely uninvited, with some off - hand remark like, "*Lo, I am with you always - even to the end of how you thought this was all supposed to be!*" or "*Let not your heart be troubled - let it be surprised!*" He'll remind me we can have further dialogue about this if I'd like. Sometimes we do. Those are rich times, that frequently take place on the page with pen in hand.

Receptivity loves quiet times of doing nothing in particular and being in the moment. She prefers our mornings unhurried, until we've spent time with the Creator and consulted with the

Wild Mama Nature, to get a sounding on the day. In my journal, she leads me through secret meadows to find a single wild violet that knows the answer to a question I'd not yet had the courage to ask. She'll catch the fragrance of a young story waiting on tiptoe, hoping fervently for a part in the next chapter of my life.

Due to her close relationship with Discernment, Receptivity to Truth is extremely skilled at capturing the remnant of something that needs to be healed. She'll bring it to me, light as a feather, and lay it in my heart. There, its pain or grief or fear can be fully felt - maybe for the first time. She waits with me while unshed tears wash over it, cleansing, clearing and allowing fresh understanding to be born. When she sees it emerging, she summons Faith and Love, who take me by the hand and teach me to care for it, lest I neglect it and allow it to die.

On the days I don't consult with Receptivity to Truth, my ordinary mind can get trapped in its squirrel cage world, and make me miserable. That's my cue to summon her.

At once, she's at my side inviting me to stillness while she designs yet another door where none existed before. Opening it, she invites me again into fresh space, filled with the Light of Heaven. There, we wait on Grace to surprise and supply us with whatever Truth we need for that day.

*I will give you the keys of the kingdom of heaven;
and whatever you bind on earth shall be bound in heaven,
and whatever you loose on earth shall be loosed in heaven.*

- Jesus (Matthew 16:19)

Sacred Journal Questions from Receptivity To Truth

1. When have you been reluctant to accept the truth of a situation? What changed?

2. Think of a time, before your own Discernment was developed, when you naively accepted as truth, something that later you had to recast in new light? (Santa Claus doesn't count. Neither does the Easter Bunny.)

3. Have there been times when Truth that eventually set you free, first made you miserable? Recount one of them here.

4. Now let Truth speak further about that here on the page, or about your response to an earlier question.

Notes

Notes

Notes

Notes

Notes

Notes

Notes

Notes

Notes

TRUST

*"It is the Lord your God who goes with you.
He will never fail you nor forsake you."*

- Deuteronomy 31:6 & Hebrews 13:5

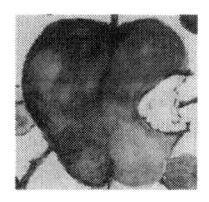

Trust

Like Creativity, Humility, Patience and the others, Trust is a spiritual faculty. His seed was placed in our soul before we were planted in our mother's womb. He sprouts readily in our young nature if we have parents that emulate the qualities of the Creator's love. Not all of us do, yet we still eventually develop Trust. His purpose is to help humanity to rely first on others, then on ourselves, and finally on the Creator's love to meet every need and solve every problem.

Trust dislikes being confused with his younger sister Faith, promptly pointing out their significant distinctions. Trust is built on personal experience, while Faith calls humans into the unknown, untried future. Trust teaches us when it's okay to try this or that, because it's worked in the past, or maybe we have watched it work for others. He teaches who we can count on and who we can't. Faith, on the other hand, beckons us into, uncertain territory and depends on Trust to develop a firm foundation for her. That's what he does best, and that's when he shines. Without Trust, Faith is slow to develop and is prone to chronic disorder.

I first learned Trust from my mother. She could always make things better when I got hurt or scared. Mom always told my brother and me that no matter what had happened, or what we'd done, we could come to her. Even if we robbed a bank or killed someone she'd say, we could still come to her. She would always love us. While neither of us robbed a bank or killed anybody, we did test and stretch that love - sometimes something fierce. Yet we knew in our bones, we could count on Mom for support and help when we needed it. Illness with alcoholism made it hard to trust Dad for much of anything. However, my brother and I learned to trust our ability to get around him when we needed to, and get things done on our own. Things didn't always turn out quite like we'd hoped, but we did pretty well.

It took me a whole lot longer to trust God as "Our Father who art in Heaven," because of our father who lived in the house. I used to pray fervently for Mom to be relieved of all the work she did, caring for bedridden grandparents, waiting tables, and putting up with dad. She seemed to me the epitome of that saintly, long suffering woman I heard preached about on Mother's Day at the Baptist church. Surely, if I just prayed hard enough, God would reward her with relief. God apparently didn't hear or didn't care. I got plenty mad at him for that, and avoided further conversation for years.

Learning whom we can and cannot trust beyond home and family gets trickier. That comes by experiment, experience, betrayal, disillusionment and disappointment. At least it did for me. Trusting ourselves, as we uncover who we really are, what we truly want gets even trickier. We're destined to be tossed out of 'paradise' more than once, until we learn higher and higher levels of Trust.

Yet Trust doesn't disappoint us. Instead, he helps us pick up the pieces and dust ourselves off, all the while gently pointing us in the direction of the Creator's Love. Eventually, if we're fortunate enough to encounter Humility, we learn to trust the Creator more than our own, limited abilities – and more than anyone else. We learn about forgiveness, grace and gratitude. We develop new levels of understanding, new ways of perceiving the events of our lives. We learn that whatever wounded us deeply, can still be healed, if we'll only let the Creator in to help.

In the year following Mom's death, I found myself sitting in the living room of the little house she'd left me. I had an awful case of bronchitis, and felt terrible. That day my chair was positioned in the same place her easy chair had sat when she was alive. Mom died with advanced emphysema. She was only 68, yet worn out from lack of oxygen and over work. As I sat coughing, wilted and miserable, I thought of her, how those last ten years of her life must have been. I asked God (whom I'd forgiven by that time), why He'd never answered my passionate teen-age pleas to help Mom!

In the silence that followed, I heard these words inside: *"Honey, your mother never asked for help. You were the one who needed help."* I promptly dissolved in tears.

Mom had accepted the way things were. She kept going and giving until she couldn't any more. It was I who railed against what I saw as her plight, then became furious at God. Because of it, Jesus had just given my inner kaleidoscope another turn. My bronchitis cleared rapidly after that.

The following spring, a friend visited from California, gifting me with a lovely crystal. Before going to dinner that evening, he wanted to meditate. Holding my crystal, I turned on a newly purchased tape. We closed our eyes and began to meditate. The music (or was it God?) invited my imagination slowly up the path of a deeply sloped mountain. On reaching the top, I was met by a lighted figure, dancing freely, joyously on a wide expanse of emerald green grass.

"Let me introduce you to your mother!" whispered Jesus, appearing next to her.

This was Mom! Long free of the painful images I still held of her life! She wanted me to be free of them too. Amid grateful tears of recognition, I soaked in that image, and tenderly took it with me back down that mountain slope as the music gently moved toward its end. Coming quietly out of the meditation, I looked on the tape jacket. It was entitled *Mother Earth's Lullaby,* by *Syncrestra (1981, Ed Van Fleet, Elfin Music Co)*. The side we'd just heard was *Slopes*. Then I realized this was March 17 - Mom's birthday!

Trust sits with me now, smiling quietly as together, we remember.

"Do you believe I am able to do this?"

- Jesus – (Matthew 9:28)

Sacred Journal Questions from Trust

1. Where did you first learn trust?

2. Where did you first experience betrayal?

3. What did you learn from that?

4. Where is your trust placed now?

5. How is that working for you?

Notes

Notes

Notes

Notes

Notes

Notes

Notes

Notes

Notes

Notes

Notes

FAITH

*"Live faith is characterized by risk and doubt.
It requires courage."*

- Paul Tillich

*"Behold, I am the Lord, the God of all flesh;
is anything too difficult for me?"*

- Jeremiah 32:27

"There is no problem in any situation that faith will not solve."

- A Course in Miracles

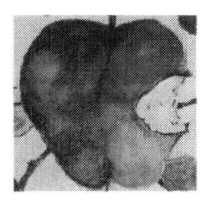

Faith

Faith wears many disguises. I once saw her downtown, posing as a lone petunia in the sidewalk crevice of the Kensington hotel. Amazed, I stopped to stare. Why would a flower choose such a place to grow? Yet there it was, dancing in the sun and breeze, without another flower in sight. Faith reminded me later that it's in the hard places, where no one else seems to be, that she's most needed. For me, that can mean the crevice between my ego's concrete ways of seeing things and a fresh possibility sprouted by the Holy Spirit, in some unexpected place.

I'd like to know Faith as that "assurance of things hoped for, the conviction of things not seen" (Hebrews 11:1-11). More often she feels like a wandering homeless woman, fragile in the face of world problems, as well as many that crop up in my own life. With enough grit and determination I can sometimes hoist on that 'full armor of God' (Ephesians 6:13-17) and imagine Faith as a shield that would protect me from whatever Goliath I currently face. But that armor feels more like it belongs to some muscle-bound Biblical warrior, than the woman I am in this life. So, when I recently got snarled in a piece of relationship drama, Faith appeared in yet another disguise. Nobody tells you this growing up, but loving relationships can push all your discord buttons. (It's probably what they're for).

In this particular snafu, I'd come to a fork in the road. No decision to make or direction to take, that I wouldn't likely later regret. Something had to change. (I didn't yet know it was me).

To quiet my tangled mind I turned inside for meditation and prayer. The deeper Self always knows what's needed next. The rational mind rarely does. It's limited to what it already thinks.

Closing the eyes and focusing on the breath is the quickest way to rein in my runaway mind. Normally I engage a mantra. But if it's still snorting, pawing the ground and stomping around, I let my imagination 'picture' the situation as I currently construe it. That gives it something to do. Then I just observe it like a stage play, from an imaginary seat in the 'theater.' That's what I did that day.

My drama promptly showed up as a thorny, impenetrable jungle with no apparent way into it. Intrigued by the image, I relaxed a little more and waited for a sense of Jesus' presence. (It always goes better when I remember to invite Him to these events). About then, a magnificent elephant popped into the scene, and stood quietly facing the thicket.

"Let me introduce you to Faith." Jesus said, appearing next to the elephant, a twinkle in His eye. "She's no stranger to this terrain Come on, get on," He added, nodding toward the elephant. "I'm going with you." Amused, I let myself imagine for a moment what that might be like. Next I felt myself astride this magnificent creature, with Jesus on behind. Faith, now disguised as a huge and powerful servant of God, methodically moved forth, pressing a path into that virgin wilderness, until the three of us disappeared in it. Left with a lighthearted sense of peaceful adventure, I got up and went about my day. Within 48 hours, the relationship issue had spontaneously transformed with humor and love.

Jesus knew what He was doing that day. An important part of Hindu worship for over 5000 years, the elephant deity Ganesha, represents divine creativity and the capacity to remove obstacles!

I next asked Faith to tell me more about her nature as a spiritual disciple. This is what she said:

"You are right that I wear many disguises. It is so with all of us who dwell in the spiritual realm. In the union between Creator and Creation, I was born the younger sister of Trust. I invite you forward into the adventurous, unknown future, based not only on past experience, but on your expanding urges, desires, hopes and dreams. These are the sources of your personal evolution. They are calls from God to become all you are created to be, to uncover and live your true potential. In this way you naturally glorify God.

"I'm both a gift from God, and a powerful servant of God. I create pathways through virgin wilderness, and open doors where there seem to be none. Your Soul knows that all things are possible with God. Yet the human mind doubts, because of its experience in the world, often at that hands of humans who do not yet remember God, or their relationship to their Creator. Think of Faith as fertilizer for the garden of your heart's desires, and the dreams God still has for your life. Then take my hand trust the Unknown."

*"I will be with you always -
even to the end of who you thought you were!"*

- Jesus (to me)

Sacred Journal Questions from Faith

1. Where did you first learn about FAITH?

2. What have you had to unlearn about what you first learned?

3. What role does FAITH play in your current life?

4. Is there anything you wish were different about that? Allow FAITH to re-introduce herself to you. There may be something to learn directly from her here on the page.

Notes

Notes

Notes

// Notes

Notes

Notes

Notes

Notes

Notes

GRATITUDE

"Seeing life symbolically means always looking for the larger and deeper meaning in any event."

- Carolyn Myss"

*I have faith in you!
Do you have faith in me?"*

*- Jesus
(as I'm working to finish this manuscript!)*

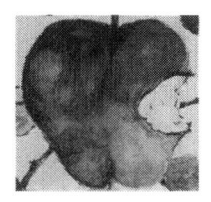

Gratitude

Gratitude is shy by nature and sensitive to her surroundings. Growing up, she was bullied by a griper who lived too close for comfort. The griper was large, loud and polluted the atmosphere. To this day, griping, grumbling and generating fear will cause Gratitude to flee for her life. The truth is, in an atmosphere fouled with mental, emotional or spiritual negativity, Gratitude can't breathe.

The younger sister of Grace, Gratitude is gentle and joyous. Yet she doesn't rise easily through a skeptical, self centered ego. She waits to be invited. That usually requires an encounter with Humility, and maybe a visit to the dwelling place of your present attitudes and past wounding.

Gratitude sprouts inside first, by being taught to be grateful when we're tiny. The child in us wants what it wants when it wants it. Being grateful is not in its repertoire. We're taught to *say* 'thank you,' whether or not we feel it, before we even know what it means. Feeling thankful inside is another story. That may not unfold until we're up against some scary possibility and waiting uneasily for the outcome. If it goes our way, we breathe a sigh of relief and feel thankful a little while. Then we take up where we left off. At this stage, in our otherwise bustling, self-centered life, Gratitude is only a sprout. The developing ego is busily focused on impression management, and worrying over tomorrow and yesterday. It rarely gives Gratitude the time of day. Being the gift she is, Gratitude will not intrude. She waits to be invited.

Gratitude is most herself when she's free to be comfortable, unhurried, imaginative and a little funky. When welcomed as a guest in the household of daily life, she'll visit readily and often. When she does, you'll start to notice first the small blessings. Then your awareness will expand to the larger gifts that God has scattered all around you. Some you've never noticed before or perhaps took them for granted. Now you breathe them in, and what you feel becomes authentic Gratitude, frequently accompanied by Humility.

Gratitude lives close to the soul and knows its innermost secrets. She loves to share a cup of mid-afternoon tea, and contemplate the present moment. If you're in a slump, she'll often suggest counting your current blessings; the ones in your immediate vicinity. While you do, she'll sweep a few more into your awareness. You'll come away lighter, more faith filled. You might even feel a silent giggle bubble to the surface.

While living in Georgia, a small group of artist-writer friends came to my tiny lake cottage for lunch. They'd heard tales about the old, wrought iron gate leading down the long, wooded lane; about the wood stove inside and the picnic table near the ravine, where much of my journal writing took place. We lunched at the picnic table, shared stories and visited the afternoon away. As supper hour approached, they called two more pals who'd now be home from work, to join us. While I loved them all, the people-pleaser hostess inside became uneasy.

The kitchen sink was full of the few dishes I had. There was little refreshment to offer two more people. Where would they even sit? What would I do? I needed a miracle! Silently I asked for help - to be delivered soon! Grace and the Wild Mama Nature heard my call.

The additional folks arrived. We all traipsed down the path so they could visit the fabled picnic table. Across the lake we noticed the sky had turned an ominous gray green. Heavy clouds roiled and rolled in the west. The wind picked up. With the scent of a developing storm in the air, we returned to the cottage.

"This looks bad," noted one of the women, "and you have all these windows! Want to come home with us, Sal?" Not usually afraid of storms, I declined. "But where would you go for shelter?" she pressed. I pointed to the small hallway between the two bedrooms. I had a little basement too, but never used it. Abruptly she exclaimed. "I almost forgot! Last night I had a dream - about being trapped in a hall just like that one! We need to leave, now! Sal please, won't you come with us?" Assuring them I wasn't afraid, I thanked them. With that, they departed for home.

Over the next twenty minutes, Mama Nature delivered a notable and much needed downpour that ceased as suddenly as it arrived.

Stepping into the fresh cool that followed, I was treated to a stunning sunset and the giggling companionship of Gratitude. Together we did up the dishes and went for a long walk. She reminded me to thank her sister Grace, and the Wild Mama who she claims, orchestrated the whole thing.

I never told my artist writer pals.

Sacred Journal Questions from Gratitude

1. Recall a time when you were secretly grateful for something that set you free, but which others may not understand?

2. Look around your immediate existence. What are you grateful for right this minute? Spend at least five minutes making this gratitude list. Then notice how you feel inside.

3. When did you learn authentic gratitude? What happened to catalyze that? Do you consciously cultivate an attitude of gratitude?

4. What do you think might change if you did?

Notes

Notes

Notes

Notes

Notes

Notes

Notes

Notes

Notes

Notes

GRACE

Grace is a dimension of God we don't recognize for much of our lives, unless someone points it out to us. Then if we're lucky, our eyes begin to open. When my mother was in the last stages of her illness with emphysema, I wanted to give to her what I'd seen her give to others. She'd cared for all four of my grandparents in their bed, until they left their bodies. I was a nurse. I wanted to do that for her. But my University teaching job required me to be out of town several days each week. I was torn with angst, when my then pastor, Rev. Dr. Robert Hurst said this to me:

"You don't yet know about Grace, Sallee. Grace is a gift from God; a gift which you can neither earn nor pay back. It is to be accepted, received and shared. Your mother's love and care for you was a gift of God's Grace. Your gift to her and to God now, is to live your life from the fullness of that Grace."

Rev. Hurst was another gift of God's grace in my life. In the year previous, he counseled me through my second divorce - before I became a member of his church.

"By grace I live,
By grace I am released,
By grace I give,
By grace I will release."

- A Course in Miracles

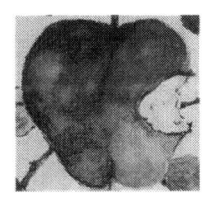

Grace

Grace is the elder sister of Gratitude and usually the first to be recognized. Gratitude quietly follows her, but only in those whose hearts have been opened. The two love to travel together and when they do, they get us through the glitches in our lives. Actually, you might not encounter Grace until you're confronted with a glitch. Humility reminds me that a glitch always stands at my growing edge.

So what's a glitch? I'll tell you what it is for me.

A glitch is any situation or event which stops me in my tracks, causing me to feel confused, conflicted, or in some kind of pain. In The Prophet, Sufi mystic Kahlil Gibran writes "Pain is the cracking of the shell of your understanding." A glitch is like that. A worthy glitch can get my ego in a hammer lock, triggering all manner of emotions that dance around like a swarm of mosquitoes or stinging nettle. My ego hates to admit this, but glitches have served a real purpose in my life. They force me to face whatever lesson I next need to learn. Still, it's hard and don't let any positive attitudes junkie tell you it's not. In the grip of a glitch you may not know what the heck to do. You may feel fragile and helpless in the face of it. That's when you need Grace.

She's always available, but sometimes (not always), you have to ask for help. Grace goes right to work, creating some minor or major miracle out of the whole thing that you would never have thought of, and couldn't have arranged anyway. I'm told this is how evolution happens. I'll tell you a true story about a glitch and Grace. This happened before I'd yet learned to ask for help from the Higher Power (s).

Shortly after finishing my masters', I was invited to present my research as a program for two district nurses' associations at a combined dinner event. The program was awarded two contact hours for continuing education. I was more than a little intimidated. Not only did I have to make it worth that, I had to cover two hours!

Working feverishly, I compiled a huge stack of note cards, along with a carefully arranged cassette of slides. The day before my presentation, I was at the dining room table organizing it all, when a friend stopped by.

A psychologist on faculty at Knox College, Gary had a huge impact on me as an undergraduate psychology major, and strongly influenced my later counseling practice.

"What're you doin' there, Sal?" he queried. Eagerly I told him. "Wow, that's great! What're you presenting?" When I replied it was my thesis research, he looked puzzled. "Why do you need all those notes?" I rushed to explain how it had to be really professional, etc., etc... "But Sal, this is your stuff! You know it by heart!" I smiled indulgently. Gary had no idea how stuffy academic nursing could be. There was no convincing him – or me - to change that day. Grace would have to do that herself. The Wild Mama would see to it that she did.

The night arrived. In the large, carpeted meeting room everyone had finished eating. I couldn't eat much. What I did swallow, sat in a wad. Hearing myself introduced, I rose. Heart pounding, mouth dry, I moved to the podium. Whatever happened next was up to me – or so I thought . . .

Diligently arranging my stack of notes, I noted the location of the power button on the projector. Unfamiliar electronic devices are always a source of anxiety to me. Adjusting the mike, I smiled, took in a deep breath and moved smoothly enough through a few opening remarks before leaning over to turn on the projector. In doing that, I 'accidentally' bumped the podium. My notes, now free of their rubber band, careened all over the floor. A collective gasp rose in the crowd. In a mix of compassion and panic, eyes darted from the scattered notes to me.

Then Grace swept in and took over. With the help of nurses near the front, the hopelessly shuffled notes were gathered and handed to me. I put them aside.

The first words out of my mouth were, 'That may have been no accident.' Everyone relaxed and I was soon loose in the water, describing the project in a way that made it professional but personal, and sometimes funny too. The audience asked really good questions afterward, and I had a good time.

When it was over, one of my pals came to me exclaiming, "Sal! That was great! And you know what? I don't usually see auras. Yet the whole time you were speaking, I saw this golden yellow aura all around you. You were in your element! You could go on a speakers' circuit."

In the weeks to come, I was indeed on a speakers' circuit of sorts, facilitating seminars in stress management. As time went on that would include invitations to conduct workshops in churches, and eventually opportunities to lead Sunday worship.

That's how Grace works. I still make notes, but rarely use them. Grace takes over, along with the Holy Spirit. Gratitude quietly follows – unless I really screw up.

*"My grace is sufficient for you.
My power is made perfect in weakness."*

- Jesus (2 Corinthians 12:9)

Sacred Journal Questions from Grace

1. When has Grace released you from a difficult situation, or state of mind?

2. What has Grace provided you without your asking? (If you can't think of anything, consider your next breath).

3. When has Grace helped you release a difficult situation, or state of mind?

4. Ask Grace to reveal how she's currently working in your life. (Don't be surprised if Gratitude shows up to join her).

Notes

Notes

Notes

Notes

Notes

Notes

Notes

Notes

Notes

WISDOM

*"The Lord possessed me at the beginning of his way
Before His works of old
From everlasting I was established.*

*From the beginning, from the earliest times of the earth,
When there were not depths, I was brought forth.
When there were no springs abounding with water,
Before the mountains were settled*

*Before the hills I was brought forth
While He had not yet made the earth and the fields,
Nor the first dust of the world.*

*When He established the Heavens, I was there.
When He inscribed a circle on the face of the deep,
When He made the skies above
When the springs of the deep became fixed,*

*When He set for the sea its boundary, so that the water
Should not transgress His command,
When He marked the foundations of the east;*

*Then I was beside Him, as a master workman,
And I was His daily delight,
Rejoicing always before Him,
Rejoicing in the world, His earth."*

-Proverbs 8:22-30

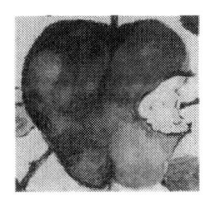

Wisdom

Wisdom knows to wait until the truth of a situation breaks through the soil of your current understanding. Her other name is Sophia. Wisdom is one of the four horsewomen of the apocalypse. (Did you know that 'apocalypse' simply means a revealing of something previously hidden, or the lifting of a veil? Or that Sophia is the Greek name meaning wisdom?) Her mighty apocalyptic companions consist of Love, Truth and Chaos.

Led by Wisdom, these four powers guide and nourish the soul development of all God's children. Yet they never force themselves on anyone. Wisdom allows her children to learn on their own, as they are ready. However, if she notices something that needs changing and changing quickly, she will summon Chaos to the scene. Chaos knows precisely what needs to be stirred to the surface, dissolved or outright destroyed; and what needs to happen next to bring about fresh, new order. When things have been sufficiently brought to light for Wisdom and Truth to enter, they are always accompanied by Love. Under the guidance of these four, new life evolves from the old. Without them, we can stay stuck for years. At least I've found it to be so.

I first encountered Wisdom as I faced a second divorce. Prior to that, I mainly followed the passions of my heart, the truth of my maverick spirit, and did my best to contain these within the Midwestern mindset of small town life. It didn't work very well. I wanted it to. But by the time I was 40, Chaos had ridden through my life in ways that made my head spin. Ragged around the edges, I secretly questioned who I was, what I was, and what God wanted of me! Why couldn't I just settle down, follow the leaders, and live an ordinary, middle class life?

Those questions needed asking then, and fairly regularly after that.

During that painful time, Wisdom would leap over logic, to bestow insights in unexpected moments. She'd waken me in the hours before dawn, urging me to write in my journal, at least long enough for her to get a word in edgewise – often on the same page. In the silence of stuff I struggled to understand, she'd whisper something like *"Be still. Learn to wait! The answer will come in its own time."*

To this day, her favorite bits of inner advice are: *"Learn to trust the mysteries,"* and *"Be still and know who is God - and who isn't."*

In those moments, I have to look at what (or who) I'm allowing to be 'God' in my life.

Over the years, I've come to embrace Wisdom as the feminine face of God. For me, she is the Wild Mama Nature, whose intelligence informs the entire Creation. That includes the laws written on my own innermost parts, and others' as well. She regularly teaches me to trust my deeper feminine Self, which at 45, I didn't even know existed.

Wisdom is one of the goddesses of enough-is-enough-already! Durga and Kali, from the Hindu pantheon are two others you might find interesting. These days, Wisdom reminds me that too much of even a good thing is still too much.

From Wisdom, I've learned I can't *always* trust my feelings. That's because sometimes they're based on thoughts and beliefs that are no longer true. Maybe they were once. Maybe they never were. Maybe they simply served a temporary purpose in my ego. In the revelation of new understanding, the old feelings gently dissolve over time. If they don't, try applying love and forgiveness.

When I've run over my own limits, which I still do on occasion, Wisdom guides me to live in day-tight compartments, and stay focused in the present. *"In the present moment is all eternity,"* she'll whisper. *"In the present moment you have everything you need. You weren't built to carry the past and the future on your shoulders."* I believe her. Still, trying to corral my ego's monkey mind in the present moment is like trying to confine a wide-awake two-year-old to its crib. It won't stay very long without a fuss.

Wisdom reveals secrets that at first are hard to believe. As an example, she steadfastly claims there is no 'death' in the way we humans think of it. It has always been so. We're all eternal, spiritual beings, at one with the Creator. We've just forgotten. She insists we come into physical form for the purpose of developing our souls more fully, and to help bring about more of Heaven on earth. Then, when that purpose is fulfilled, we merely transition out of these body forms.

I guess we're still learning to do this business of bringing about more Heaven to Earth. Yet when I see TV news - and what passes for entertainment – that's sort of hard to swallow.

Wisdom insists however, that the Kingdom of Heaven is perfectly united and perfectly protected, and our ignorance, evil and folly will not prevail against it. She wants us all to know she's still our Mama, and that she's here to guide us, as we each take our part in bringing about more Heaven right where we are.

Meanwhile my task is still learning how to love more freely and fully, to forgive myself and others, and not to judge according to my ego's perceptions. Wisdom adds that the Creation isn't yet finished – and your piece is needed too!

Sacred Journal Questions from Wisdom

1. What have you learned from Wisdom in your own life? How has she come to you?

2. When have you experienced the Four Horsewomen of an apocalyptic event or time in your own life? What did these four teach you?

3. When (if) you (can) imagine Wisdom as a feminine aspect of God, how do you respond to that?

4. Invite Wisdom to speak to you on the page for a few minutes. You may want to consult her about a specific matter.

Notes

Notes

Notes

Notes

Notes

Notes

Notes

Notes

Notes

Additional Food for the Wildish Soul

*"While some women find spirituality within religion,
Others need to make a distinction between the two."*

- Joan Borysenko

Additional Food for the Wildish Soul

Several years ago, while wrestling with the patriarchal language of Christianity, Wisdom gave me this version of Psalm 23. If it's helpful to you, she'll be delighted. Who knows? She may have another version just for you!

Sophia's Psalm for Sallee

The Goddess is my shepherdess, I shall not want.
She makes me to lie down in the green pastures of my mind,
and leads me beside the still waters of my soul,
to restore my truth to me.

She leads me in paths of right-use-ness
for her Holy namesake.

Even when I walk through the valleys
of darkness, debt, depression and disillusionment,
anger, fear or hurt of any kind,
I will fear no evil, for She is with me.
Her wisdom and her truth, they comfort me.

She prepares a table before me in the presence of my enemies,
and anoints my mind with fresh insight.
My cup of understanding runs over with Her blessings.

Surely goodness and mercy DO follow me all the days of my life
And I will dwell forever in the house of
My Heavenly Father, my Elder Brother Jesus,
and the Wild Mother Goddess, Sophia.

Acceptance
A Visit to an Unusual and Inexpensive Retreat Center

Acceptance is the daughter of Wisdom, and a younger sister of Intuition. Acceptance is quiet, wise, and easy to be with, once you've decided to surrender to what is – whatever it is! That's not always easy.

I first learned about *The Retreat Center of Acceptance* when I was in sore need of a vacation from the pressure of too many unfinished tasks, too much self-doubt and other stuff I couldn't do anything about. I'd known for some time I needed to let go of a large chunk of what I'd been doing for the last 20 years. That was hard. It had been part of my identity. People counting on me to continue as I had been were in for a surprise. I didn't have any rational explanation -- except it was time to do something different, to move in some new direction, though I hadn't a clue yet what that was. As the Earth Mama turned toward her Winter Solstice, the days grew darker, the nights longer, both inside and outside of me.

One particularly cold, dark morning, with snow falling on snow, I finally became still enough, long enough to let Intuition find me. She whispered that her sister Acceptance, operated a retreat center by the sea, and suggested I make a reservation.

The week between the Christmas and New Year's holiday was the perfect time for such a trip. Long weary of the forced frenzy and commercial folk festivals around winter holidays, I find creative ways to escape. I've secretly had my most splendid and memorable holidays doing just that. But that will be saved for the next book! Meanwhile, I sent for more information on *The Retreat Center of Acceptance*, and made a reservation. Come along if you'd like.

The Retreat Center of Acceptance is a rambling old mansion by the sea, as ageless as the sea itself, with too many rooms to count. Anyone is welcome, at any time. However, advanced reservations are required. Acceptance insists on that. She also strongly encourages you to stay for at least seven days the first time you visit. It's the only way you'll get what you truly came for, which is spiritual direction from the inside. Besides, she requires time to prepare for your visit, to assure that when you do arrive, the other guests there at that time will be completely compatible.

Acceptance arranges things so you'll not only be comfortable, you'll also receive the food your soul most requires, and on whatever schedule is most needed for recovery from wherever you've been.

Within an hour of your arrival, you'll feel yourself unwinding from the worldly schedule of activities and clock time. You'll discover a subtler, more natural rhythm within; one you may never have known was there. You'll learn to eat only when you're hungry, and to stop when you've had enough. You'll sleep until you waken naturally, regardless of what clock hands indicate. You'll learn to live more and more, in the present moment and enter fully into the unfolding, eternal 'now'. After two or three days you'll become an "outlaw" to the world's ways of going, doing, scheduling and planning – and your soul will rejoice. By that time, you'll have begun to uncover the other set of laws - those sacred, natural laws, written on your innermost parts by the Creator, before you were formed in your mother's womb. Acceptance will help you accept these laws, in place of those you made up (or were made up for you by the world into which you were born).

At *The Retreat Center of Acceptance* you'll take long walks by the sea of your soul, and discover treasures washed up by the tidewaters of your deeper consciousness. You're encouraged, to gather a few of these into whatever container you brought with you. A journal, a sketchbook, a canvas, a pocket; even your bare hands will do. Upon your return from the sea, you can lay them out like an oracle, on the altar of your unfolding truth.

Suspending all judgment, notice what they reveal.

Notice how you feel about that.

Acceptance will look on with you, gently blessing each revelation. The truth that sets us free, often regurgitates stuff our ego would rather avoid.

In these few days of sacred retreat, you'll learn more fully who you are now, what really matters most, and how best to live that out in the world to which you return. Be patient with yourself. Most of us who come here the first time are not able to shed our old skin all at once. Lasting, authentic change comes slowly. The emerging Self beneath must be nurtured, developed, and strengthened from inside. This requires time, trust, patience, and several more visits to *The Retreat Center of Acceptance.*

A bonus blessing of such a retreat is there's no huge financial price tag! The only requirement is your willingness to reserve the time, let God and other intelligent beings in your life run the world for a few days, and make the inward journey. You don't even have to leave home! I didn't. (You can send the others away, bury your cell phone, and turn off the ringer on your land line!)

So the next time you're in need of renewal, schedule a week - or at least a long weekend - at *The Retreat Center of Acceptance.* It's a place you'll want to visit again - and again. If you're anything like me, you'll probably need to. It's a delicious way to begin a new season of your life, and to give thanks and reflect on the one you've just lived. You'll be glad you did.

This was given to me during meditation, as I prepared the Sunday message to be delivered at the Unity Church of Quincy, IL – Fathers' Day, 2005.

Papa's Love Letter

I am the God of History. I am also the God of your story.

I call My people out of their history and into the present, where their unfinished story awaits its glory, in My name.

The journey to the Promised Land is not a long one, child. All it requires is taking My hand and stepping out of the story you erroneously created, when you discover it is not one befitting a child of God. Then let Me guide you to your true and rightful inheritance as My child.

Do not be afraid of My laws or My guidance, for both were written on your innermost parts, long before I knit you together in your mother's womb. It is that Law and that Love that will bring you fully into your True Self, which glorifies Me. As with any father, My greatest joy is seeing My children ripen into their full glory.

> I am not remote, nor hard to find.
> I am the silence between your words.
> I am the breath that rises and falls in your bosom.
> I am the wind that stirs the trees, and the Spirit that ripens the grain.
> I am the Great Spirit.
> I am the Great Mystery . . . The Creator of all that is . . . and
> I am your Papa. I am their Papa too . . . Tell them that.
>
> Love,
> God

Repeat these words slowly to yourself.
Let their meaning wash over your mind.
Feel the transformation happen inside.

The Divine Love Prayer

Divine Love is doing its perfect work, here and now.

Divine Love illumines.

Divine Love harmonizes.

Divine Love revitalizes.

Divine love adjusts.

Divine Love rejuvenates

Divine Love transforms.

Divine Love provides.

Divine Love heals.

Divine love guides.

Divine love prospers.

Divine love forgives.

Divine love foresees everything, and richly provides every good thing for this relationship/situation now.

Author Unknown

The Royal Society of Successful Quitters

Sometimes I think I'd like to organize the Royal Society of Successful Quitters. Timely quitting is a little known, overlooked, sometimes castigated art. Yet for any spiritual warrior, it's an art of necessary cultivation. Successful quitting requires enormous courage, great humility and considerable strength of character. Quitting in a culture such as ours is not popular. We value hanging on at all costs – even when what you're hanging on to has been DEAD for years! Sometimes we hang on to places and people that are positively poisonous, priding ourselves on how much immunity to poison we've developed, out of imagined virtue and sheer will power! We hang on - instead of holding out for what we really want. We hang on and 'make the best' out of impossible situations, because we're afraid to let go – and let God - lead us to where all things are possible again – or at least more of 'em.

I love people who quit when it's time. They simply honor their limits and move in another direction, whether they know quite where they're going or not. I feel especially tender toward those innocent souls who, certain they have failed or fallen short, still couldn't have remained one more day where they'd been. They may have had an intolerable wedlock that had become a deadlock. Or an abusive job that nevertheless, had 'wonderful benefits'. Yet their soul couldn't say. So come hell or high water (and it's often both at first), they let go and went their way, not knowing what that way would be. That takes faith! Raw, radical, life-giving faith! Faith in the Great Unknown. This is the faith of the young eagle. After weeks of tenuous branch walking, and practice flapping of its untried wings near the nest where it was raised, it makes the life changing leap into flight.

Only then can the invisible winds of fated change waft beneath it and carry that pilgrim across the Grand Canyon or Royal Gorge of the next life space. There's no way to know ahead whether one can do it – until one lets go. Such timely leaps into the Unknown, in service of the Soul's growth, are the mark of Royal blood. It belongs in its own Royal Society.

A Contemporary Swedish Hymn
By Tore Littmark
(Recently translated into English)

Dare to question, dare to test things.
Dare to seek, search, unconfined.
God's embodied in your questions
Already God has you in mind.

Dare to question, dare to feel doubt.
Dare to take the path you chose.
God's already deep inside you,
Closer than you dare suppose.

Dare to question, dare to say 'no'.
To far too simple, glib replies.
Dare to wait and dare to waiver.
God will still be at your side.

Dare to question, bold and fearless,
God will still believe in you.
Life in you is God's own purpose.
Already God has you in view.

Dare to question, doubt and wonder.
You are loved by God, retrieved.
You are longed for, seen discovered,
Free to live and to believe.

This was sent via e-mail from a recent conference attended by Episcopal Bishop John Shelby Spong, author of RESCUING THE BIBLE FROM FUNDAMENTALISM

Resources for Tending the Soul Garden

> *"By listening to each other, and to themselves,*
> *women can heal their spiritual wounds*
> *and forge new, intensely personal*
> *connections to the divine."*
>
> *- Joan Borysenko*

In addition to my well worn *New American Standard* Bible, *A Course in Miracles*, *The Unity Metaphysical Bible Dictionary*, and my current copy of Unity's devotional, *Daily Word*, I keep the following resources close to my bed. They continue to nourish my soul and provide perennial wisdom. If you are a spiritual seeker, I recommend them all. Many can be opened randomly to any page to discover something you needed to see, even if you'd read it before. If you haven't, you'll likely want to, and be glad you did. They're placed here in the order I took them from the shelf.

Estes, Clarissa Pinkola - *Women Who Run With the Wolves- Myths and Stories of the Wild Woman Archetype*: New York, Ballantine Books, 1992. Dr. Estes is a lyrical writer, storyteller, scholar and brilliant analyst of Jungian psychology. In this epic work she identifies an archetypal pattern within the psyche of every woman, which she named 'the Wild Woman' archetype. Dr. Estes likens a healthy woman to a healthy wolf – robust, inventive, playful, loyal and when necessary, fierce. In each of twenty teaching tales from around the world, she traces various aspects of women's soul development, including the leg traps and poison bait we often encounter. She also points us to the ways we recover and learn to endure and to thrive. *(A great resource for workshops or retreats!)*

Cameron, Julia – *The Artist's Way – A Spiritual Path to Higher Creativity:* New York, Putnam Publishing Co., 1992. This is a beautifully written twelve week program for resurrecting, empowering and stimulating your creative life, regardless of its expression, or how long it has lain fallow. It's full of inspiration and practical, do-able exercises – for you and your inner child!

Pearson, Carol S. – *Awakening the Heroes Within-Twelve Archetypes to Help Us Find Ourselves and Transform Our World:* New York, Harper Collins, 1991. Pearson identifies twelve archetypal patterns that guide the lives of both men and women, whether we know it or not. *The Innocent, the Orphan, the Caregiver* and *the Warrior* help us build an ego, a self image, a way of being in the world. *The Seeker, the Lover, the Destroyer*, and *the Creator*, push us into taking our soul journey, where we discover the treasure of our true Self. *The Ruler, the Magician, the Sage* and *the Fool* enable us to bring that treasure of the true Self forth, to transform our own lives, and the world around us. Each of these archetypes has a major task, a major fear, three identifiable stages of development, and a major gift. She also has a test you can take to see which of them are currently most active in your life! *(Another great resource for workshops or retreats!)*

Quigley, Sarah with Shroyer, Marilyn – *Facing Fear and Finding Courage*: Berkley, Conari Press, 1996. This little book offers gentle, inspiring support for negotiating the dark waters of fear and anxiety that happen to us all from time to time. The short, easy chapters guide us step by step through a three-fold process of facing, feeling and transforming fear. You'll learn that fear is a 'message' not a 'monster', and the secret fertilizing ingredient for growing a reliable crop of courage. A second edition, ***The Little Book of Courage- A Three Step Process for Overcoming Fear & Anxiety*** came out in 1996 by the same publisher.

Bancroft, Anne – *Weavers of Wisdom-Women Mystics of the Twentieth Century*: New York, Viking Penguin/Arkana 1989. Bancroft explores the teachings and methods of fifteen modern women mystics, each of whom has developed her own approach to spirituality. Individually and together, they give a lovely and freeing view of the wise, deep approach to the sacred world beyond the veil of our five senses. A must read for any woman who has spiritual experiences, or soul longings that don't quite fit her traditional religious environment

Moore, Thomas – *Care of the Soul-A Guide for Cultivating Depth and Sacredness in Everyday Life:* New York, Harper Collins, 1992. Moore guides us to view life from the eyes of the soul, more than our socially conditioned surroundings. He suggests we honor symptoms, such as depression or pain, as messengers rather than simply something to be silenced or medicated; that we learn to find treasure in the small events, and mundane tasks of everyday life. He guides to in creating rituals that give meaning and depth to changes in our lives, and to develop a more soulful balance between work and money. *(Keep this book by your bedside stand for those times when your soul wakens you in the night, because that's the only time it's been able to get your attention!)*

Borysenko, Joan – *A Woman's Journey to God*: New York, Riverhead Books, 1999. If you are a woman who has had to abandon the religious beliefs you were raised with, to seek a more authentic spiritual path for yourself, this book is a must read! Borysenko is a highly respected medical researcher in the area of mind-body health, and a leading authority on feminine spirituality. You'll be fascinated and fed by what she shares here, from the retreats she leads, and from her own spiritual journey.

Spong, John Shelby – *Rescuing the Bible from Fundamentalism: A Bishop Rethinks the Meaning of Scripture* (New York, Harper San Francisco, 1991). If you're interested in the Bible, yet you're unable or unwilling to believe in literalist interpretations, John Shelby Spong's book will help. Written for lay people by this brilliant contemporary scholar and compassionate Christian thinker, John Shelby Spong invites us to an adventure with the Bible and an expanded view of Christianity; one that frees us to find new meaning there, and in our own relationship to it. He's written many books, and has a great website.

Powell, Robert – *The Sophia Teachings-The Emergence of the Divine Feminine in our time*: New York, Lantern Books, 2001. Powell takes us on an illumining journey to discover how Sophia, the Divine Feminine, became lost to Western culture and buried, with the rise of the patriarchal Roman church. Now, in our time, she once more rises to the surface to take her rightful place in the collective human consciousness. *(Great for understanding the rise of feminine influence and Sophia's much needed wisdom in these times.)*

Beyondananda, Swami with Steve Bhaerman – *Driving Your Own Karma-Swami Beyondananda's Tour Guide to Enlightenment:* Rochester Vermont, Destiny Books, 1989. Need laughter? Humorist, Steve Bhaerman's *Swami Beyondananda* will crack you up, with tales of his 'vision quest' with Chief Broken Wind, and how his 'clown chakra' opened in a New York subway, en route to see his guru, Harry Cohen

Baba in the garment district You will learn patience with the Swami's Wait Training Program, how to heat your home with anger using Tantrum Yoga, maintain your car with Swami's Auto - Suggestion techniques, and recover from Oughtism. This little book will guard you from the dangers of terminal seriousness and may open your own clown chakra too! Find it and other pathways to "eternal laugh", at his website, *www.wakeuplaughing.com*

Young, Wm. Paul – *The Shack: Where Tragedy Confronts Eternity* (Newberry Park, CA, Windblown Media, 2007). This powerful story blurs the line between 'fiction' and the Reality that exists beyond the veil of our ordinary consciousness. What happens to *Mack* after the abduction and murder of his beloved five-year-old *Missy*, will dumbfound and entertain you. It includes a visit from God as *Papa, Jesus* and *The Holy Spirit*, that will blow open your heart-mind, and dissolve barriers to a personal relationship with God. You can read this book in a weekend, but you'll want to share it with a discussion group. Our church tried to cover it in eight weeks, but we couldn't stop. It went on for 16 weeks!

Moffatt, Betty Clare – *the Authentic Woman-Soulwork for the Wisdom Years*: New York, A Fireside Book/Simon & Schuster, 1999. This little book is written with clarity, humor and wisdom. Offering comfort, inspiration and advice for the challenges and joys of the third phase of our lives, its short chapters and authentic tales make it soul food for the woman over fifty.

Bolen, Jean Shinoda – *Goddesses in Every Woman- A New Psychology of Women*: New York, Harper & Row, 1984. If you've not explored the archetypal patterns in us as women, this would be a good place to begin. Psychiatrist and Jungian analyst, Dr. Shinoda-Bolen describes seven 'goddesses' from the Greek pantheon, whose energies, whether or not we realize it, inform and influence our lives as women. You'll learn about *Artemis*, goddess of the hunt and the moon; *Athena*, goddess of wisdom and craft; *Hestia,* goddess of the hearth and home; *Hera*, goddess of marriage; *Demeter*, goddess of grain and maternal instincts; *Persephone*, perpetual maiden and queen of the Underworld; and *Aphrodite,* goddess of love and beauty. Women waking up to who they really are will find themselves aligned with one, several or most of these 'goddesses'.

Bolen, Jean Shinoda – *Goddesses in Older Women-Becoming a Juicy Crone*: New York, Harper-Collins, 2001. There are several goddesses who do not emerge into full expression, until a woman is over fifty. We have been 'maidens' and 'mothers'. However, crossing the threshold into the 'crone' phase of our life ushers in powerful new energies often not available at earlier stages. Dr. Bolen identifies the goddesses who enter during what she calls Act Three. Included are: *Sophia*, goddess of wisdom now hidden in the Bible; *Durga* and *Kali*, Hindu goddesses of transformative wrath (when 'enough is enough!); *Hecate*, goddess of the crossroads of our lives; and *Baubo*, goddess of healing laughter. If you are a woman over fifty, this book will ignite fires of illumination that inspire and enrich your life during Act Three.

Whitcomb, Holly W. - *Seven Spiritual Gifts of Waiting*: Minneapolis, Augsburg Books, 2005. We all need to learn how to wait! Holly Whitcomb gives us practical instruction in this little known art! A United Church of Christ minister and retreat leader, her delightful book is an easy read, and excellent resource for an adult education class at church. That's where I first used it. We all benefited. The seven gifts of learning to wait are *Patience, Loss of Control, Living in the Present, Compassion, Gratitude, Humility* and *Trust in God.* She offers exercises with each that deepen the spiritual life, along with inspiring stories from her own life.

Chopra, Deepak – *The Third Jesus-The Christ We Cannot Ignore*: New York, Harmony Books/Random House, 2005. I always knew Jesus would sooner or later get hold of Deepak Chopra! I've read nearly everything Chopra has written. This is a crowning work. This book bridges a much needed gap between the historical Jesus, the Jesus taught in church, and Jesus as the living Cosmic Christ. This living Christ is a spiritual guide whose teaching Chopra says, "embraces all humanity". He adds, "Jesus speaks to the individual who wants to find God as a personal experience . . ." and points out all through this fascinating book, how Jesus invites us, all through the scriptures, to search for the Kingdom of Heaven within. You'll find fresh meaning in Biblical scripture interpreted by Deepak Chopra. From all the praise on the book cover by highly respected contemporary Christian figures, it appears Chopra has done his homework.

LaMott, Anne – *Plan B-Further Thoughts on Faith*: New York Riverhead Books, 2005. In Ann LaMott, I found another left-wing, maverick Christian sister, who thinks and speaks from a liberal perspective with a bent toward finding peace and creating social justice. I was first introduced to Ann LaMott by a woman pastor friend, who lent me *Traveling Mercies.* I now read everything I can find by Anne LaMott. She is hilariously funny, deeply human and gut-level honest as she tells of her own dilemmas, faith, foibles, alcohol addiction and life as a single mother of a now teen age son.

*"The Lord God will cause righteousness
and praise to spring forth
before all the nations."*

- Isaiah 61:11

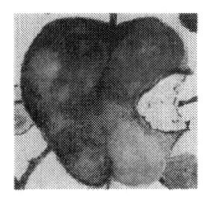

About the Author

Sallee belongs to a secret Native American tribe known as the *Yougottawanna's*, and is a founding member of *The Royal Society of Successful Quitters.* She had found *The Road Less Traveled* long before she read Scott Peck's book by that title.

A life-long spiritual seeker and left-wing Christian maverick, Sallee believes God is still speaking to us - no matter what our faith – if we're simply willing to listen! She maintains that the Christianity of Jesus (as distinguished from *'Church-ianity'* and religious extremism), offers us three things: the courage to be our true self - the ability to define that self in the world - and to live that life in freedom. It also includes reverence for the Earth, love for others, and respectful willingness to learn from other traditions.

Ten years as an emergency room nurse ignited a passion to help people care for themselves more healthfully, more naturally and more soulfully. With an undergraduate degree in psychology and a master's in nursing, she became a founding member of the American Holistic Nurses Association in 1981. In 1982, she left a stint of university teaching to embark on a solo private practice as a clinical specialist in stress management. Believing the mind and body to be inseparable from the soul and spirit, she quickly added massage therapy, hatha yoga classes and meditation training to her services. Over the past 30 years, she's led retreats, seminars and continuing education programs.

Following a second divorce, Sallee turned to personal journaling to sort through her experience. There she 'accidentally' discovered a gentle, yet powerful method of accessing what's hidden in the heart. She calls this process *Sacred Journaling.* The soul's wisdom longs to be given a voice. When tapped, it can and will guide us to find creative solutions from within ourselves.

Sallee has led yoga classes and journaling workshops in a variety of church settings and enjoys filling in at the pulpit wherever there's an opportunity! While living in Georgia she considered seminary at Emory University - until she learned from three respected pastors, that she'd be required to declare a denomination early, and spend the next three years defending it. (Sallee *still* doesn't know what 'denomination' she is! But she figures Jesus might have the same problem).

So it was back to *The Road Less Traveled,* where she remains an 'itinerant preacher of the practical gospel for wild hearted souls', and offers journal seminars aimed at finding our right relationship with ourselves, with God as we understand God, and with the others in our lives - however different that may be from what we learned growing up – or at church!

Sallee now lives in her home town of Galesburg, Illinois, where she's a member at First Presbyterian Church (unless they throw her out after reading this book).

Made in the USA
Charleston, SC
13 March 2011